English Silver

English Silver

Judith Banister

Paul Hamlyn

LONDON · NEW YORK · SYDNEY · TORONTO

The original Italian edition

Gli Argenti Inglesi

© *1966 Fratelli Fabbri Editori, Milan*

This edition © *1969*
The Hamlyn Publishing Group Limited
Hamlyn House,
The Centre, Feltham,
Middlesex

Text filmset in Great Britain by Yendall & Co. Ltd,
London

Printed in Italy by Fratelli Fabbri Editori,
Milan

INTRODUCTION

People have not been collecting silver—old silver, that is—for very long. As a subject for the art collector and historian, silver is only some 70 or 80 years old. Pictures, furniture, sculpture, bronzes, china, jade and other objets d'art were sought by the 18th-century connoisseur, but silver, except for an occasional piece, usually medieval or continental in origin, was not. Silver was something to be bought for use or display. It was in fact considered as so much capital in a pleasant, useful form.

If a man had a good storeroom of plate, he had at the same time a good private bank balance. Silver went into the melting-pot if the owner wanted a new house, or perhaps a new coach, or even new clothes or a dowry for his daughter. More often it was turned into cash if the government unfortunately began to press for payment of taxes or duties. But while it was a source of bullion, it was also there to be used, and silver was *de rigueur* at the dinner table and, later, at the tea table and breakfast table as well, by all those who considered themselves to be gentry or people of taste from the 17th century onwards.

There was nothing very vulgar about showing off one's silver to the neighbours, much as one would nowadays take them to see a new car or swimming pool. Samuel Pepys, the hardworking and garrulous civil servant whose *Diary* tells us so much of life in the England of Charles II, wrote with obvious pride in 1667:

'We had, with my wife and I, twelve at table, and a very good and pleasant company, and a most neat and excellent—but dear—dinner. But Lord! to see with what way they looked upon all my fine plate was pleasant; for I made the best show I could, to let them understand me and my condition, to take down the pride of Mrs Clarke, who thinks herself very great.'

Pepys was not averse, either, to taking a piece of plate along to the goldsmith's shop to have it melted and made into something more fashionable.

Perhaps the surprising thing is that so much old silver has survived. A lot is the accumulated wealth of great or old-established families. In times past, a present of silver was one of the ways that a man could express gratitude for services rendered. In addition, those families of which a member had acted as an ambassador overseas, at least from the mid-17th century until 1815, usually obtained the ambassadorial plate, which might weigh up to 4,000 oz., as a perquisite of the office.

Presumably also, the growing wealth of the middle and merchant classes saved quantities of plate from being melted during the 18th century and later. Since the civil wars of the early 17th century, when King or Parliament took all they could get from the strongrooms of their supporters, there has been no large-scale destruction of plate in England. Only radical changes of taste or the ravages of wear and tear have from time to time condemned it to the melting-pot, or, especially in the early 19th century, showered it with ill-conceived ornament. Today, almost every piece, large or small, with or without historical or even aesthetic appeal, is saved by a whole world of silver collectors. Only hard use, and too heavy a hand with cleaning agents, remains the enemy of old English silver today.

Fortunately, silver is durable as well as beautiful. Provided that the gauge of the ware is heavy enough, a well-made piece of silver will stand up to many decades of use. As it ages, indeed, its lustre—the soft grey sheen known as patina—improves it to a beautiful dulled brilliance, so that age enhances, rather than detracts from its beauty.

The same is true of silver-gilt. Old silver-gilt is often a lovely pale, lemon yellow. Unhappily, much modern gilding is bright or dark yellow, and pieces that need regilding—especially salts and wine cups—are sometimes spoiled by electrolytic gilding. The old method, done by driving off mercury from a gold and mercury amalgam, was injurious to the health of the worker. Electrolytic gilding, both quicker and safer, can, of course, be matched to any colour of gold, but all too often too little attention is paid to such details.

Incidentally, references in old books or inventories to 'gold' plate often mislead people into supposing that in the past there were vast quantities of gold plate in existence. In England the term 'gold' usually meant 'gilded' and was used loosely in contrast to 'white', which was used for ungilded silver. In some of the more stately country houses there are still separate strongrooms for 'white' and 'gold'.

In style, English silver is almost always unmistak-

1. Mazer bowls. 1510 and *c.* 1460. Diameter $5\frac{1}{4}$ in. The Worshipful Company of Goldsmiths, London.

2. Standing salt. 1542. Height 9¾ in. The Worshipful
Company of Goldsmiths, London.

1. Mazer bowls. 1510 and *c.* 1460. Diameter $5\frac{1}{4}$ in. The Worshipful Company of Goldsmiths, London. Bowls made of the spotted maplewood and mounted with silver or silver-gilt provide some of the most delightful of late medieval and Tudor wares. Known as mazer bowls, they usually have a deep lip mount and nearly always also have a small raised medallion in the centre often with an engraved or enamelled print. Inscriptions in Gothic lettering were not uncommon as on the right-hand mazer. The left-hand one has two bands of repeating cast ornament around the rim, and the print, showing traces for former enamelling, is chased with a Tudor rose.

2. Standing salt. 1542. Height $9\frac{3}{4}$ in. The Worshipful Company of Goldsmiths, London. An early example of the beginnings of Renaissance decoration in England is this octagonal standing salt. The shallow receptacle of the salt is enclosed within a cup-like section reminiscent of late medieval hourglass salts, but the bracket supports and the finial of Hercules holding a serpent and shield indicate Renaissance motifs.

3. The Bowes cup. 1554. Height $19\frac{1}{4}$ in. The Worshipful Company of Goldsmiths, London. One of the rare survivals of an exceptionally fine silver-gilt and rock-crystal standing cup is the Bowes cup, a magnificent example of repoussé chasing and cast chasing. Four tiny figures of Atlas support a crystal bead in the stem, while the cup itself is a crystal cylinder supported by four caryatids. The domed cover is richly chased with strapwork, fruit and masks, from which rises a bracketed finial topped with the figure of a female carrying a shield bearing the arms of Sir Martin Bowes who presented it to the Goldsmiths in 1561. It is traditionally Queen Elizabeth I's coronation cup.

4. The Gibbon salt. 1576. Height $11\frac{3}{4}$ in. The Worshipful Company of Goldsmiths, London. So important was salt at the table that it was sometimes enshrined in a masterpiece of architectural form. The Gibbon salt, which was presented to the Goldsmiths on St Bartholomew's Day, 1632, by Simon Gibbon, was made in 1576. Four Ionic columns enclose a central cylinder of rock crystal in which is enclosed a figure of Neptune supporting the cellar. Four small cupolas are arranged above the capitals of the columns, and the central dome of the cover is surmounted by a tall urn finial.

3.　The Bowes cup. 1554.

4. The Gibbon salt. 1576. Height 11¾ in. The
Worshipful Company of Goldsmiths, London.

ably English. One can look at a piece and say, 'That is English, probably made in London, about 1720' (or 1700, or 1780 or whenever the style suggests). That judgment can then, usually, be verified by the hallmarks which identify not only the maker, but also the place of making, the standard of silver used and the year it was made.

But while English silver has its own special characteristics, it can only rarely be said that a piece is entirely English in form and decoration. In fact, almost all the silver made in Britain has borrowed something from abroad. Ever since the Renaissance spread slowly northwards to reach the England of Henry VIII about 1520, there has been wave after wave of continental influence on English silver. Assimilating each fashion as it crossed the Channel, the English silversmiths of each period interpreted it to create the distinctive and definitive designs that are the charm of English silver.

The styles of English silver during its greatest years —from about 1650 to 1830—appear in a readily datable series, making the study of design both interesting and rewarding. The dating of this progression of styles is, of course, immensely assisted by the remarkably orderly system of hallmarking. This had its origins more than 600 years ago, and the great majority of English silverwares are hallmarked. There are exceptions—notably pieces made to special order which were not 'set to sale' in shops, and the marking of many provincial pieces is sometimes haphazard. But even unmarked or partly marked silver can usually be dated with confidence, and in many parts of the country, students are doing research on the makers of the provinces.

Apart from the built-in documentation of the hallmarks, however, English silver is but very poorly served by records. There are lists of makers and their apprentices in the books kept by the Worshipful Company of Goldsmiths in London, and sometimes lists in the larger provincial centres. Occasionally old ledgers are found giving details of pieces made, their weights, sometimes their makers and their buyers, and the prices charged. But of the individual makers, there is rarely little more known than the odd date or two—his birth, perhaps, the year of his apprenticeship, his Freedom of the Goldsmiths' Company, and perhaps an obituary notice. Clothing the bare bones with a portrait, family papers or other information is mostly impossible. Only by their wares, which survive as records of their skills, and by their individual marks, most of them now identified, can the silversmiths of Britain be known.

FROM THE REFORMATION TO THE RESTORATION

Because so little silver made before the middle of the 17th century survives, the year in which Charles II was restored to the throne, 1660, is usually judged a good starting point for tracing the history of silver styles in Britain. Pre-Restoration silver is rare, and therefore now predominantly destined for museums, unless it happens to be part of the fairly extensive collections of plate in the possession of City livery companies, colleges and universities.

Indeed, because of its rarity, even the changing fashions in silver are difficult to trace much before 1650 or so. Apart from spoons, which do survive in reasonable numbers, there is little purely domestic plate. That is, of course, due partly to custom, and partly to the relatively few rich families who owned any silver at all. Even a well-to-do burgher would probably have no more silver than a few spoons, perhaps one or two drinking cups and maybe a salt. Those, as the traveller William Harrison noted in 1587, 'of the degree of barons, bishops or upwards' would have many more silver vessels, such as grand cups, salts and goblets, but even so most of these were for show as much as for use.

Some inkling of the great wealth of plate of the 15th and 16th centuries can be gleaned from the collection of early English silver in the Kremlin, Moscow, many items of which are unparalleled in English collections. But even by Elizabethan times much fine silver and some gold as well had been melted when Henry VIII dissolved the monasteries. Iconoclast though he was, Henry was himself a great and extravagant patron of the arts. He appointed Hans Holbein his court goldsmith, and though no known piece designed by him is extant, there are a number of drawings recording the magnificence of the plate made for the King.

It appears that most medieval and Tudor silver was made under the design influence of Germany and the Low Countries. Pattern books used by goldsmiths all over Europe appear to have been international in appeal, but it is unwise to be dogmatic about this in view of the scanty number of pieces surviving. The earliest known piece of silver that shows the Renaissance to have reached England is the Boleyn cup, belonging to the church at Cirencester. It is dated 1535, and the graceful fluted trumpet-shaped cup has the cover surmounted by a falcon, the badge of Queen Anne Boleyn. But it was the end of the Gothic period

5. Salts. *c.* 1600 and *c.* 1690. Victoria and Albert Museum, London.

6. Standing cup. 1599. Height 10½ in. The
Worshipful Company of Goldsmiths, London.

5.   Salts. *c.* 1600 and *c.* 1690. Victoria and Albert Museum, London. The small circular salt on the left has a gadrooned edge in the Baroque manner. Silver-gilt, it is unmarked, but dates from about 1690. The salt on the right is a very rare Tudor trencher salt of triangular form on three cast mask feet, the upper surface embossed and chased around the central circular well.

6.   Standing cup. 1599. Height 10½ in. The Worshipful Company of Goldsmiths, London. This typical late Elizabethan gilt standing cup was presented in 1613 to Sir Hugh Myddelton to commemorate his work on the construction of the new river to improve London's water supply. The cup is oviform and is flat-chased and engraved with shells, foliage, flowers and strap-work. Three finely cast and chased scroll brackets decorate the baluster stem.

7.   Ceremonial salt. 1601. Height 22 in. The Worshipful Company of Goldsmiths, London. By the end of Queen Eliza-beth's reign the ceremonial standing salt had generally become rather simpler and was usually either cylindrical or bell-shaped. This unusual drum-salt makes use of a rock crystal cylinder to display a parchment roll showing the arms of the Goldsmiths' Company and an escutcheon inscribed 'Ric. Rogers, Comp-troller of the Mint'. The salt was given by Rogers to the Gold-smiths in 1632. It is richly chased with foliage, and the small steeple finial on three caryatid brackets rises from a faceted crystal ball.

8.   Pair of silver-gilt dishes. 1601. Diameter 8 in. Private col-lection. These shallow Elizabethan dishes have broad reeded rims. The centres have applied circular bosses bearing the engraved coats-of-arms, very much in the style of the applied discs in the centres of wooden mazer bowls.

7. Ceremonial salt. 1601.

8. Pair of silver-gilt dishes. 1601. Diameter 8 in.
Private collection.

in England, the age of the hourglass salt and the font-shaped cup, of which, happily, a few remain in college collections at Oxford and Cambridge and in museums around the country.

The age of ceremonial silver was far from extinct, however. Standing cups, great goblets, flagons and tankards, ewers and dishes, and a wide variety of great salts were all part of the Elizabethan goldsmiths' repertoire. An increasingly wealthy merchant class also meant a growing demand for lesser silverwares, notably mounted wooden and pottery bowls and jugs, small cups and beakers, trencher salts and of course spoons. These were made with various finials, from apostles and lions sejant to acorn knops and seal-tops.

When Queen Elizabeth died in 1603, the House of Stuart came to the throne, in the person of James VI of Scotland. On reaching his new capital, James must have been overcome with a sense of power on seeing the royal treasures. Though so near, Scotland and Scottish customs were extraordinarily different from those of England, and within a few years James had managed to deplete it by making lavish gifts of it to foreign powers, notably Castile.

His son Charles I turned what was left to his own insatiable requirements for money, and when civil war split the country, both factions took their toll of what was left from public and private treasuries alike.

The civil war not only wrested silver from its owners; it also brought to a stop the making of silver-wares, other than a few essential spoons, bowls and church pieces. For more than ten years, the trade was virtually in abeyance. After the parsimonious years of the Commonwealth, it was hardly surprising that when Charles II was restored in 1660 the silver-smiths were among the first to rejoice.

England in 1660 was a land where civil war and its aftermath had wrought many changes. The ill-fated Stuart claims to the divine right of kings, the growth of the middle classes in the struggle for more democratic government, and new and far-reaching developments in science, industry, trade, overseas enterprise and in architecture and the arts had made the transition from the traditional, almost feudal life under the Tudors to the beginnings of modern Britain. In fact, the country was over the teething troubles of social revolution a full century before most of her continental neighbours.

After the frugal years came a great upsurge of spending. Estates were restored to the royalist supporters, new houses were built, and filled with modern furniture and with all the good things being imported, such as porcelain and carpets, and the new products, such as flint glassware. The silversmith was also much in demand. But the interregnum had wrought havoc in his workshops. There were few master silversmiths capable of sustained high quality work, especially in the ornate manner which the patrons had come to approve during their long exile on the Continent. The bold flowery styles, usually of Dutch origin, were not easy to execute, and silver was, despite huge demands, in very short supply. It is not, therefore, to be wondered at that many silverwares of the 1660s and 1670s were rather flimsy and somewhat crudely worked. And the unending orders for cups and tankards, porringers and caudle cups, salvers, dishes, toilet services and even silver-mounted furniture at least had the advantage of keeping the silversmiths busy; and, being busy, they soon learned to handle their tools and their designs better, and even to develop their own sense of style.

Two-handled bowls or cups, usually known as porringers but also sometimes called caudle cups (because
it was believed they were used for the spiced wine and
milk favoured as a panacea for minor ills at the time),
are among the most typical of mid-17th-century silverwares. They had almost straight-sided or else bellied
bowls, and were provided with handles on either side
because the drinks and foods served in them were
usually hot. The bellied style was at first decorated
with matting and lobed ornament, but soon the exu-
berant flowers, foliage, birds and animals popular in
Holland at the time made their début in London. The
decoration was usually embossed and repoussé chased,
which helped to conceal the fact that the metal was
rather thin. A favourite pattern in England featured a
lion on one side and a unicorn on the other, all of
course in a forest of scrolling foliage. The handles of
these cups, which vary in size from an inch or two to
as much as 7 or 8 inches in height, were usually cast,
and many took the form of scrolling caryatids. Some
also had covers, usually domed.

The return of the monarchy heralded a return to
ceremony, though not again on the pre-civil war scale.
Some of the standing cups, especially those sur-
rendered by corporations of towns or cities, were replaced, and occasionally standing salts were made
once more—mostly capstan-shaped, the small semi-
circular cellar held in the waist of the spool, which
featured three or four supports round the top to hold,
presumably, a napkin cover.

In fact, silver for display was usually in the form of
vases and jars suitable for arranging along the mantel-
piece, in the Dutch style, and more rarely in the form
of furniture. Nell Gwynn is said to have had a silver
bed made for her in 1676, and there are silver tables at

Windsor Castle and at Knole in Kent. Silver-mounted hearth furniture was also made, which must have looked very splendid gleaming in the firelight.

The Restoration period also saw the earliest surviving silver candlesticks and sconces. Again, at first, Dutch styles predominated, and the candlesticks usually had square or hexagonal bases, fluted or cluster column stems, and very large drip pans. Sometimes the stems and bases were more highly decorated.

Morning visits were a fashionable pastime, and those who called upon My Lady in her bedroom could see her magnificent toilet service, with anything up to twenty or thirty pots, caskets, boxes, candlesticks, bowls, pincushion and mirror, and even perhaps small cups from which she could take some soothing beverage. Most were understandably rich in style, and most were gilt.

The greater skills of the silversmith, as demand for his work increased, can be gauged from the variety of techniques employed. The rather coarse embossed decoration of the early period gave way to more meticulous, though still flamboyant, repoussé work, with scrolling foliage hiding chubby amorini, birds, animals and swags of fruit. A rare technique found on pieces made about 1670 and lasting until about 1685 was to sheath a piece of plain silver gilt with a pierced and chased silver sleeve.

Quite soon after the Restoration, some silversmiths had already begun to find other sources of inspiration than the Dutch pattern books. For those who did not like or could not afford richly ornamented silver, contrasting matted and plain surfaces were popular, and simple engraved strapwork and foliate scrolls followed a tradition originating in the last years of Elizabeth I.

9. Ming ewer with English silver mounts. Formerly in the Spencer-Churchill Collection.

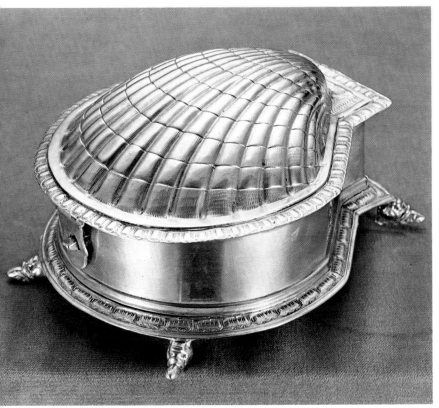

10. Small sugar or spice box. 1620. Length 6 in. Ashmolean Museum, Oxford.

11. Saucer-dish. 1634. Diameter 8 in. Private collection.

9. Ming ewer with English silver mounts. Formerly in the Spencer-Churchill Collection. Oriental porcelain, as well as less exotic pottery, was frequently mounted with silver during the 16th and 17th centuries. This Ming porcelain ewer has English silver mounts dating from about 1610. There is a similar example in the Victoria and Albert Museum. Photograph courtesy Christie, Manson & Woods Ltd, London.

10. Small sugar or spice box. 1620. Length 6 in. Ashmolean Museum, Oxford. Small boxes, probably used for sugar or spice, were usually shell-shaped between about 1595 and 1625. Most had four cast shell feet, or more rarely, snail feet, as on this box. It has typical stamped decoration round the edge of the cover and foot, and a latch fastening.

11. Saucer-dish. 1634. Diameter 8 in. Private collection. Large numbers of saucer-dishes—usually called strawberry-dishes because the fruit was much esteemed at the period—were made during the 1630s and 1640s. Although two exactly alike are rare, most were similar, with eight fluted panels embossed with formal flower heads and beaded punchwork. A large proportion of these dishes were the work of William Maundy, who made this one in 1634.

12. Silver-gilt flagon. 1646. Height 10 in. Victoria and Albert Museum, London. This flagon was made in 1646 by a maker who marked his work with a 'hound sejant'. He was invariably a fine worker, at a time when the craft was largely in abeyance because of the Civil War. This flagon is silver-gilt and chased overall with panels of dolphins and sea-monsters on a foliate and flower decorated ground. Its pair is at Temple Newsam, Yorkshire.

12. Silver-gilt flagon. 1646.

From France the silversmiths learned the technique of 'cut-card' work, in which thin sheets of silver are cut into decorative shapes, notably scrolls or foliage, and applied neatly round the bases of bowls and tankards, or round the junctions of spouts, handle sockets, and finials. Cut-card work also had the advantage of strengthening the silver as well as ornamenting it.

Between about 1670 and 1685, a naïve but amusing and rather charming style came into fashion, especially for personal silver such as toilet sets and caudle cups. It is known as *chinoiserie,* and was apparently only favoured in England at this time. Perhaps it was inspired by the tales of the orient brought back by English merchants and sailors. The designs seem to be the armchair imaginings of a land of Cockaigne, full of strange and exotic temples and houses, long-robed figures and wide-winged birds, palm trees and flowers—curious pictures of a world that was offering Europe new pleasures and treasures beyond the age-old spices and silks: rare porcelain, and, of paramount importance to the silver trade, a new beverage called tea.

Tea, coffee and chocolate were all introduced into England about 1650, and quickly took their place in society. Suitable silverware, since most pottery was coarse and imported porcelain very expensive, was at once in demand, and having no precedents the silversmiths adapted the ubiquitous flagon, giving it a spout and a side handle. The style proved only a passing one for teapots, which were by the 1670s made after the style of Chinese winepots, no doubt on the recommendation of oriental travellers. For coffee and chocolate, however, the tall tapered cylinder was to be the standard shape for more than half a century.

With a few rare exceptions, silver for tea, coffee and chocolate was relatively plain. So were many drinking vessels. Wine cups of silver really made their final appearance during the Charles II period, for it was during his reign that Ravenscroft's development of flint glass became a commercial proposition, and only rarely did a patron now require silver goblets for his wine.

Not so with beer, however. Tankards were made in huge numbers, and of huge capacity, often holding as much as one or even two quarts. The bodies were usually straight-sided, tapering slightly towards the stepped flat cap cover, which was hinged above the scroll handle. A cast thumbpiece, in the form of a double scroll, a corkscrew or, on occasion, a more decorative motif, such as a lion sejant or a bird, was often the only concession to decorativeness. The owner's initials, if he had no coat-of-arms to be engraved on the body, are often found on the handle or on the base of tankards of the period. The old 'skirt' foot of the Commonwealth tankard gave place to a narrow rim foot, sometimes reeded, or, more rarely, to three cast feet, in the forms of lions, pomegranates or birds, in the Scandinavian manner.

To 'save the carpit or the cloathes from drops' the salver came into use during the 1660s, sometimes made *en suite* with the tankard or the caudle cup. It was often equally plain, and usually stood on a trumpet-shaped foot.

The traditional bellied mug and the tapering beaker continued to be made in large numbers all over the country. Beakers were usually cylindrical, tapering slightly to the rim, and standing on a narrow reeded or moulded rim foot. Small and simple, often relatively heavy small cups with no handles and rounded

13. Wine-cup. 1657. Height 7¼ in. Harvey and Gore, London.

14. Saucepan. 1657. Diameter 4¾ in., height 3¾ in. Private collection.

13.   Wine-cup. 1657. Height $7\frac{1}{4}$ in. Harvey and Gore, London. This exceptionally large and fine plain wine-cup of the Commonwealth period was made in 1657. It stands on a sloping circular foot and the baluster stem supports a large straight-sided bowl with slightly everted lip. It is inscribed 'The Gift of John Hutham Barnett & Michell Warton E^r Buriesis [Burgesses] for the toune of Beuerley & Giuen to the Company of Buchers Anno Dom 1661.'

14.   Saucepan. 1657. Diameter $4\frac{3}{4}$ in., height $3\frac{3}{4}$ in. Private collection. Early silver saucepans were direct copies of those in base metal. This silver skillet was raised from a single sheet of silver and stands on three feet. The applied shield opposite the scroll handle is engraved with a coat-of-arms, and probably acted as a stop for the cover, now missing. Later saucepans had baluster-shaped bodies with flat bases, short lips and turned wood handles.

15.   Salver. 1660. Diameter $15\frac{3}{4}$ in. The Worshipful Company of Goldsmiths, London. Continental styles of repoussé work very much influenced the English silversmiths starting work again after the lean years of the Commonwealth. This fine footed salver has a broad rim embossed and chased with hunting scenes. The depressed centre is beautifully engraved with a contemporary coat-of-arms in a plumed scroll and floral mantling. It was made in 1660 and is considerably heavier than most pieces of the period, weighing 44.5 oz.

16.   Ceremonial salt. c. 1662. The Worshipful Company of Goldsmiths, London. When the diarist Samuel Pepys went to Portsmouth in 1662 as part of the delegation meeting Queen Catherine of Braganza, he was shown the splendid spool-shaped salt to be given to her by Portsmouth Corporation. Four great eagles with wings displayed and four small hounds seated on orbs decorate the flat top with the well for the salt. The central part is of rock crystal, while the stepped base stands on eight small lions couchant. On the base are cherubs' heads with wings displayed and bands engraved with flowers and foliage. When the Queen returned to Portugal in 1692 she apparently sold the salt to the goldsmith Thomas Seymour, who presented it to the Goldsmiths' Company.

15. Salver. 1660.

16. Ceremonial salt. *c.* 1662. The Worshipful Company of
Goldsmiths, London.

bases, called 'tumbler cups', were made in large quantities, presumably for spirits or other strong drinks. Sometimes these were made in pairs, the rim of one fitting into its partner (double cups).

Since beakers, tumbler cups and tankards were essentially functional, most are quite simple in style. The early plain types were made throughout the period, but matting generally gave way to embossed decoration about 1675, especially in the west country, while in Norwich and East Anglia engraved strapwork was more often used.

In London about 1680, a new formality began to creep into silver design. Again the inspiration was Dutch—the gadroons and flutes, the formal acanthus decoration and the repeat borders that tidied up the flourishes and the asymmetry of the first years of Restoration silver. It was a formalising much needed for many of the wares now being made in silver—for casters for sugar and spices, for example, now much more plentiful than ever before in the history of Britain; for the small sets of two, four, six or eight trencher salts that had by now everywhere (except at civic and other high ceremonies) replaced the great salts; for the cups and covers with handles either side that must have been used on every grand occasion in even moderately wealthy households, and certainly at weddings, christenings and funerals; for rich, but less gaudy, toilet sets; and for severe columnar candlesticks, for tall flagons, for great tankards and, of course, for tea and coffee pots.

This new formality coincided also with a new influx of designers and silversmiths. The Huguenots, fleeing from religious persecution in France, found in England a safe refuge, though not always a warm welcome. But when they did manage to establish themselves among the jealous craftsmen of London, they brought to the craft of the silversmith a new corpus of skills, techniques and designs that were to make English silver of the first years of the 18th century the most sought after of all wrought plate of any country and any period.

THE HUGUENOTS AND THE HIGH STANDARD

Prosperous England, with her fight for freedom of the common man won, and with a growing trade at home and overseas, must have seemed a haven of peace and plenty to the persecuted Protestants of France. For many years since the Roi Soleil had dominated the throne with his autocratic rule, the plight of the Huguenots had been worsening. Most of them were of the artisan classes, and as new oppressions overcame them, more and more fled to countries where personal liberty was better respected—to Holland and Germany, England and America. In 1685 Louis XIV revoked the Edict of Nantes that had until then given them some measure of toleration. His act turned the trickle of refugees from France into a torrent.

In England the first Huguenot silversmiths had arrived about 1680. In 1682 two of them, one being Pierre Harache, a craftsman of exceptional skill and ability, were admitted to the Freedom of the Goldsmiths' Company. Freedom of the Company was necessary for any master goldsmith who wanted to set up on his own and to register his mark. But the silversmiths of London were jealous of their craft, and frankly inimical to the prospect of strangers in their midst. This became even more pronounced when they realised that many of the Huguenots seeking admission to the trade were men of outstanding ability, and that their designs and techniques were just what their patrons were finding most to their taste. The Huguenot craftsmen were acceptable to them only so long as they were not free to work on their own, but had to take jobs as workmen in the shops of the London silversmiths.

This state of affairs could not, however, continue for long. One by one, the Huguenots managed to break down trade opposition to their applications for Freedom of the Goldsmiths' Company. Some were sponsored by leading citizens, some became Freemen of other Companies. By the end of the century, names such as Daniel Garnier, John Chartier, Pierre Platel and David Willaume had joined that of Harache and his son in the registers of the Company. The Huguenots were making their impact on the history of English silver.

Many of the immigrant Huguenots came, not from Paris, but from provincial towns and cities where the latest whims and fashions of the court had had less effect. The French styles they brought with them were, perhaps to Parisian eyes, a little outmoded. In England, they added just those essentials lacking in late 17th-century silver design. Their styles appealed to even the most vociferous of the London goldsmiths who opposed them. They were fine craftsmen, who chose to use metal of heavy gauge and, when decoration was required, they executed it with meticulous detail. Their greatest merits lay in their appreciation of detail, and their fine sense of proportion and form.

In form, their introduction of the baluster shape

17. Ginger jar. 1663. Height $17\frac{1}{4}$ in. S. J. Phillips Ltd, London.

18. Two-handled cup and cover. 1668. Professor Derek Jackson Collection.

17.   Ginger jar. 1663. Height $17\frac{1}{4}$ in. S. J. Phillips Ltd, London. Silver for show in the second half of the 17th century very largely consisted of vases and jars made as garnitures for the tiered fireplaces fashionable at the time. This silver ginger jar is one of a pair and is repoussé chased with acanthus foliage beneath festoons and pendant swags of fruit and foliage. Cast cherubs' masks rise from chased wings on the shoulders below more chased swags surrounding the cover. The pair weigh 224.5 oz.

18.   Two-handled cup and cover. 1668. Professor Derek Jackson Collection. This cup and cover in the Charles II style is embossed and chased with scrolls, shells and foliage. Made in London, it bears the maker's mark 'BECG' in monogram. Owned by Professor Derek Jackson, son of Sir Charles Jackson, to whom this porringer and its pair, now in the National Museum of Wales, once belonged.

19.   Porringer. 1668. Victoria and Albert Museum, London. Made in York, this small two-handled cup, usually called a porringer, is embossed and chased with flowers and foliage in the Dutch manner, and with scrolling cast caryatid handles of stylised form.

20.   Cup and cover. *c.* 1670. Private collection. Not all Charles II cups and covers were decorated with repoussé work. This fine heavy example, weighing over 28 oz., has a cylindrical body, decorated round the base with formal cut-card work— a technique introduced from France about the middle of the 17th century. The snake motif loop handle on the cover is also French in style. The cup bears the arms of Ralph Cotton and his wife within a typical plumed cartouche. It bears only the maker's mark 'HW', presumably having been made to special order.

19. Porringer. 1668.

20. Cup and cover. *c.* 1670. Private collection.

was perhaps the greatest contribution of all. They rid the silversmiths' shops of the squat, bulging-bodied cups with their emaciated caryatid handles. They ousted coarse embossing, disorderly foliage, and the humorous but ungainly animal motifs and naïve *chinoiseries*. Out went the fluted columnar candlestick; in came the elegant baluster. They turned straight-sided flagons into helmet-shaped ewers with flying scroll handles. They made two-handled cups taller, with bell-shaped bodies on stepped moulded circular feet, and gave them bold harp-shaped or scroll handles. And everywhere, in form and in decoration alike, they paid attention to formality and detail. Flowerheads and diapers, strapwork and baluster motifs, foliage and flutes were harnessed and orderly. A riot of acanthus foliage became a neat repeat leaf border, swirls became formal flat flutes, and the only animals seen were dignified lion masks.

It would be unwise and unfair, however, to credit the Huguenots with too much influence on English silversmithing. The English silversmiths of the 1690s were already achieving greatness in their handling of the Baroque, and the Baroque continued in favour alongside the new Régence styles from France well into the reign of Queen Anne. Significantly, however, some wares remained the province of the often rather conservative English masters—notably tankards and other silver for beer and ale, which even twenty years later were not often made in quantity by French-born silversmiths. On the other hand, helmet-shaped ewers and the rare shallow écuelles were not made by English-born craftsmen, and without so much as a glance at the maker's mark, one could in such cases easily determine the nation-ality of the maker.

Meanwhile, the British government was taking a none too benevolent interest in the craft. So great was the demand for silver that not a few silversmiths, it seems, were melting down the coinage to obtain enough metal. In March 1697 an 'Act for encouraging the bringing in of wrought plate to be coined' reversed the process, and certainly caused the destruction of some plate sent to melt by unwitting owners. All new wrought plate, moreover, had to be made of a new higher standard silver, 'marked with the figure of a woman commonly called Britannia'.

The new law may have prevented the coinage from being melted, but it in no way abated the demand for silverwares, and the years of the Britannia standard, from 1697 until 1720, are among the most productive in the history of English silver.

Silver of the period is frequently plain, relying for its appeal on the grace of its form and the beauty of its own soft grey lustre. This plainness has nothing to do, however, with the fact that Britannia silver is softer than sterling, as has at times been suggested. The higher standard metal takes decoration extremely well, and was used, even after 1720 when it was no longer obligatory, for many exceptionally fine and highly decorative pieces, especially by Paul de Lamerie, who continued to use the higher standard continuously until 1732.

Nor, on the other hand, is all Queen Anne and early Georgian silver plain. Many splendidly decorated examples were made, often emulating the French Régence style. Rich chasing in low or high relief, intricate detail in the applied strapwork, fine cast and chased decoration, and superb engraving, especially for the Baroque cartouches enclosing coats-of-arms, were all very much the order of the day. But whether it was enriched with ornament for those who could afford it, or plain for those with more restrained tastes and slenderer purses, almost all the silver made in London in the last decade of the 17th century and the first quarter of the 18th century was graceful, dignified, and well balanced.

The period saw still more changes in social habits, with less silver made specifically for display, and very much more for everyday domestic use. Tea, coffee and chocolate were vying with wine and beer, punch and other beverages, but whatever the choice, the fashionable world demanded that it should be served in silver.

At the beginning of Queen Anne's reign it was estimated that there were some 450 coffee houses up and down the land. They were a centre of business as well as social life, a hub of news and gossip and, of course, tremendously important in spreading the fashion for drinking not only coffee, but chocolate and tea as well.

Silver coffee pots were part of the silversmith's stock-in-trade from about 1680 onwards. The typical pot was a straight-sided tapering cylinder, holding about one pint of coffee. Usually it was circular in section, but during the first decade of the new century it was sometimes octagonal or, more rarely, hexagonal. A rim foot followed the outline of the body, and the cover, mostly high domed and topped with a baluster finial, followed suit. There had for a while been a tendency to make the covers conical, but the fashion had gone out by about 1700. The straight spout also went out of fashion between about 1690 and 1700, to be replaced by the graceful 'swan-neck' spout. This sometimes had its own tiny hinged cover, but by the reign of George I (1714-1727) this had given way to the 'duck's-head' terminal, a slightly

21. Tankards. 1678 and 1667. Prof. O. Richmond and the Ashmolean Museum, Oxford.

22. Drinking cups. 1679 and 1681. Ashmolean Museum, Oxford.

21. Tankards. 1678 and 1667. Professor Oliffe Richmond and the Ashmolean Museum, Oxford. Late 17th-century tankards were almost always very capacious, and usually relatively plain. That on the left, 6 in. high, has repoussé chased acanthus foliage encircling the foot—a motif repeated in a most unusual way on the cover below the double corkscrew thumbpiece. The bold scroll handle is beaded and is pierced below. These holes allowed the air to escape when the handle was being soldered to the body. The front of the tankard is engraved with a coat-of-arms in plumed mantling. Similar plumed mantling shows off the arms on the plain earlier tankard on the right. This has a typical scroll handle with double-lobed thumbpiece. The hallmarks, which also appear on the body, can be seen struck across the flat cap cover, as was usual at the period.

22. Drinking cups. 1679 and 1681. Ashmolean Museum, Oxford. A variety of small drinking cups was popular during the late 17th century. The small mug on the left, with a thistle-shaped body and reeded ribbon scroll handle, was made in 1679. It is $3\frac{3}{4}$ in. high. Equally popular were the small cups known as 'tumbler cups'. This little example (centre) is 2 in. high and $2\frac{1}{2}$ in. in diameter. On one side it is inscribed 'A tous Nos Amis' and on the other 'Bevez tout'. The so-called College or 'Ox-eye' cups are peculiar to the Oxford and Cambridge colleges. This cup (right), 3 in. high, weighs nearly 8 oz. and is inscribed with a reference to Magdalen College and to the University of Oxford. It was made in 1681.

23. Candlesticks. 1682. Height $10\frac{1}{4}$ in. Ashmolean Museum, Oxford. Typical late 17th-century candlesticks on square stepped bases, with fluted column stems and broad square drip pans.

23. Candlesticks, 1682.

overlapping section half covering the top of the spout. Handles were of turned wood, sometimes leather-covered, and were set either at right angles to the spout or opposite it. Less often, horizontal handles in the continental manner appeared on coffee and chocolate pots.

In style there is little difference between the pots for chocolate and for coffee. Probably many were used for either beverage, but for the dedicated chocolate drinker there were special pots with hinged flaps in the cover through which a stirrer-rod could be inserted to whip up the thick mixture to a froth.

Within the apparent limitations of coffee and chocolate pot design the silversmiths managed to make many variations. One of the most effective was the use of intricate cut-card work applied round the junctions of the handle sockets and of the spout. Faceted spouts were popular, and the base of the spout was often scalloped. A few, mostly of English workmanship, had fluted and chased decoration on the bodies, and even applied silver straps along the tops of the handles.

Tea by the reign of Queen Anne was no longer a drink taken primarily medicinally. It had become a fashionable morning drink, though for some years it was drunk plain, without milk, cream or sugar. Its price remained high for many years, so that early teapots are usually small. The earliest known was made in 1670, but looks like a coffee pot, and would be so described were it not for a contemporary inscription recording its use. The next style of teapot followed the style of Chinese wine pots—and looked more like a posset pot for hot spiced concoctions than a teapot. But by about 1700 the teapot had settled down to a fairly modern shape—the delightful squat pear-shape, with high domed cover, curved spout and often as well a small tripod spirit lamp or brazier. Sometimes the fashionable octagonal shape was produced for the teapot too, but only very exceptionally was any other piece actually made *en suite* with the teapot or coffee pot. Towards the end of Queen Anne's reign, however, the practice of taking milk or, more often, warmed cream with tea, and also sugar, introduced the very first services, of which one or two are known, consisting of teapot, cream jug and covered sugar bowl.

Another innovation at the tea table was the tea kettle, and this, often provided with its own lamp and stand, obviated the need for teapot braziers. The pear-shape was used for the kettle during the Queen Anne period, but it became rather more globular during her successor's reign. The large swing handle was usually insulated with a turned wooden section, and some kettles were even provided with special salvers or trays, called tea tables.

A silver canister to hold the tea was hardly an extravagance when tea was so very expensive, and they were sometimes made in sets—one for black tea, one for green tea and another for sugar. Square, oblong or octagonal in outline, they usually had a bottle-like top with a domed cover through which the hostess could pour the tea. The caddy was usually filled from the base, which was sliding.

Silver teacups and stands were also sometimes made, but they must have been hot to hold, and more practical, though extremely rare, were frames and saucers for porcelain cups.

Milk and cream gradually came to be served with tea, and very small baluster jugs, with or without covers, made their appearance at the tea table. They were often miniatures of the large jugs made for beer and wine, with a circular baluster body on a moulded circular foot, and with a bold scroll handle. The cover was usually domed and provided with a baluster finial. It might extend over the lip, or the lip might have its own small hinged flap cover. A variant was the egg-shaped jug on tripod feet with a high domed cover and scroll handle, usually of wood, opposite the spout.

When sugar was taken with tea, the bowls were often fairly small, generally quite plain, and had a domed cover with rim top which, inverted, could act as a stand for the tongs. Small oval or oblong trays, sometimes fluted at the edges, were used to hold spoons.

For ground sugar at the dining table the caster that had been introduced in the late Charles II period was easily converted from the plain cylinder to the baluster form. Plain or octagonal, with a slip-on cover instead of the rather clumsy bayonet fixture of the previous century, the pear-shaped caster became a vehicle for some of the most delightful piercing, with arabesques and tiny flowers and even, in one most beautiful example, with tiny figures carrying sugar bags among the piercing. Indeed the craftsman's consummate skill at piercing, using only hammer and chisel, was typical of the superb craftsmanship of ancillary workers in the silver trade—the engravers, the piercers, the flat chasers and the casters, all of whom worked to exceptionally fine limits and with painstaking skill seldom equalled since then.

Sugar was crushed in the kitchen and then served from casters. Smaller matching casters were used for mustard, which was at that time served dry, and for spices. Mustard casters were often fitted with unpierced sleeves so that the powder could not be sprinkled by mistake over the food. Certain spices

24. Salt. 1695. Height 2½ in. Victoria and Albert Museum, London.

25. Travelling set. Private collection.

26. Covered mug and plain mug. 1702 and 1707. Height of plain mug 4¼ in. Private collection.

24.   Salt. 1695. Height $2\frac{1}{2}$ in. Victoria and Albert Museum, London. A small capstan-pattern salt with gadrooned foot and rim, and simple punched motifs at base of body.

25.   Travelling set. Private collection. This travelling set still has its original shagreen leather case. The beaker is engraved with a hunting scene. Inside fits a velvet-covered block holding a tiny octagonal double spice or salt box, a knife, fork and spoon, with detachable handles and with screw ends to hold smaller items—a toothpick, three napkin hooks, a nutmeg grater. There is also a seal-ring with a sheathed corkscrew in the handle. The beaker was made in 1702 by Charles Overing, the other pieces by smallworkers.

26.   Covered mug and plain mug. 1702 and 1707. Height of plain mug $4\frac{1}{4}$ in. Private collection. The covered mug has a pear-shaped body, spirally fluted at the base with punchwork above and with another band of punched decoration below the moulded rim. The scroll handle has a beaded spine, and the loose domed cover is fluted and features a rosette of cut-card work below the baluster finial. Though made by David Willaume in 1702, the mug is typically English in style and was in fact copied from an earlier example of 1688. By the early 18th century the large covered straight-sided tankard was less fashionable, but the similar type of cylindrical mug continued to be made alongside the Huguenot-influenced baluster mugs. This fine small mug was made by John Jackson.

27.   Punch bowl. 1704. S. J. Phillips Ltd, London. Large bowls for punch were among the most notable objects of late 17th-century Baroque silverware. Many of them had notched tops, usually removable, over which the glasses were said to be hung. These bowls are usually called 'monteiths' after a 'fantastical Scot' who lived in Oxford and was said to have worn a scalloped cloak. Monteiths followed most of the late 17th-century styles, sometimes being decorated with *chinoiseries,* sometimes decorated with cross-fluted panels. After 1700 straight fluting was more usual, but Baroque motifs were perpetuated in the shaped mounts, the lion-mask and ring handles and the bold scalework and foliate cartouche. This monteith was made by Samuel Wastell.

27. Punch bowl. 1704.

were ground and served in casters (sometimes called 'muffineers') or in small covered boxes. These were really little caskets, often with two divisions, and sometimes also with a tiny section for grating nutmeg in the centre.

For salt, small so-called 'trencher salts', placed beside each plate, were circular, octagonal or hexagonal in outline.

Casting was much used, and with considerable skill, for candlesticks, and for handles, spouts, finials and applied ornament. The typical candlestick of the early 18th century was baluster-shaped, usually on a square base with cut corners, with a circular well above the moulding of the base, and the circular knops rising to the vase-shaped sockets. Some of the protruding sections might be gadrooned, especially until about 1705, and some had tiny lion masks applied at the shoulders. By about 1710 the central well often disappeared, and the base rose to the stem, which was by now often a little taller. Faceted bases helped to give the candlesticks of the period added elegance, and also greater reflectivity. The average table candlestick was between 7½ and 10 inches high, but for the toilet table much smaller versions, perhaps only 4½ inches high, were made. For the writing table there were pairs of tapersticks, miniature sticks for the small wax candles used to heat sealing wax.

Wall sconces were still made for the more extravagant households, the backplate now usually elongated, with one or two candle branches. No doubt, too, there were a few silver chandeliers, but the 18th-century patron of the arts, though lavish in his spending, never bought such luxuriously showy pieces as the silver furniture of the late Charles II period. His display pieces, except for cups and covers, which were still made in large numbers, were primarily useful —large wine cisterns and wine fountains, usually made by Huguenots in the impressive Régence style, punch bowls and great tankards, mostly the work of the native London silversmiths, and often retaining Baroque forms and decoration well into the reign of Queen Anne, and fine silver and silver gilt for the dining table—dishes, tureens, dessert stands, etc.

The ewer and basin still had its place at the dining table, for though forks were already more plentiful, they were still not always used. Even in the last years of the century, Fanny Burney the diarist noted that they were only used for special occasions. The helmet-shaped ewer, with its flying scroll handle often in the form of a figure or with a lion mask terminal, and with the lower part of the body enriched with applied work and masks, was a speciality of the best Huguenot craftsmen.

Of less pretentious style were the large baluster jugs used for beer and wine, mostly quite simple, with a moulded rib round the body and a double-scroll handle. Some had low domed covers and scroll thumbpieces, and all were beautifully sturdy and usually of good gauge silver.

The cup and cover, with handles on either side and a bell-shaped body standing on a moulded circular foot, was one of the chief items of display silver made. The 'Huguenot' style of cup and cover was rather taller than that fashionable in the Baroque period, and though some were quite plain, relying for their appeal on the simplicity of a moulded rib round the body, double-scroll handles and a domed cover with baluster finial, others were exquisitely decorated with applied work—palm leaf motifs and strapwork in low relief, and tiny medallion heads and rows of husks growing up from the bases which themselves were often chased with gadroons, ovolos and guilloche borders.

Elegantly engraved coats-of-arms, enclosed within fine Baroque cartouches, were both indicative of the ownership of the piece and highly decorative as well. A few of the engravers of the period have been identified, among them Hogarth (who was apprenticed to a silversmith but did not, in fact, remain in the trade for very long), Joseph Sympson, Simon Gribelin and Benjamin Rhodes. They and their fellow engravers revived the art in England, as their colleagues likewise attained high skill at chasing and at casting. Sadly, few of the engravers and other craftsmen can be identified. But for the collector, there is the pleasure of being able to identify the actual maker of the silverware. The attributions of marks, which before 1697 have so often to be tentative, can nearly always after that date be ascertained from the Goldsmiths' Company records.

The new styles that swept through fashionable London, coinciding with the enforced use of Britannia standard silver, mark the beginning of the great era of English silversmithing. There was a growing insistence on good quality and a growing market for all kinds of silverwares. The higher price of the Britannia silver does not appear to have reduced the demand for domestic wares, though the silversmiths naturally fought hard to have the ancient sterling standard restored. This was eventually done in 1719—with the sting in the tail of so many Acts: a new tax, of 6d an ounce on all wrought plate. New wares continued to pour forth from the shops, and London silversmiths, busier and busier, vied with one another to produce new styles and new ideas for their customers. With a second generation of Huguenot craftsmen in their

28. Sugar casters. 1705. Height 8¼ in. Ashmolean Museum, Oxford.

28.   Sugar casters. 1705. Height $8\frac{1}{4}$ in. Ashmolean Museum, Oxford. The baluster form was early adopted for the sugar caster, especially by silversmiths of Huguenot origin, who also favoured applied or flat-chased ornament and designed intricate, pierced patterns for the tops. These large casters are a pair by Lewis Mettayer. The outward-curved baluster form is eight-panelled and chased with strapwork on a matted ground. An unusual feature is the method of securing the scroll-pierced cover, a slip-lock being used to obviate the usual clumsy bayonet clamps. The casters are each engraved on the bases with their original weights—20 oz. 8 dwt and 22 oz. 17 dwt—instancing the heavy silver of the period.

29.   Cup and cover. 1705. Height $9\frac{3}{4}$ in. Ashmolean Museum, Oxford. A superb example of a cup and cover by the Huguenot silversmith, Pierre Platel. The bell-shaped body is mounted on a circular gadrooned foot, and is decorated with applied chased straps of alternating designs. The harp-shaped handles are especially typical of Huguenot work, and the low-domed cover is enriched with cut-card leaves and a beautifully modelled bud finial. The cup is engraved with the arms of Lady Mary Boscawen and Hugh Gregor, and an inscription recording her gift of the cup to the son of her friend Elizabeth Gregor.

30.   Inkstand. *c.* 1705. Length $10\frac{1}{2}$ in, width $5\frac{1}{4}$ in. Private collection. An elegantly simple inkstand, on four bun feet, with depressions for pens and wafers. The drum-shaped pot for ink has a small hinged cover, while that for pounce is simply punch-pierced in a geometric pattern. The stand was made by Isaac Liger, whose mark appears four times on the base.

31.   Table basket. 1711. Victoria and Albert Museum, London. In this table basket, by Thomas Folkingham, the sides are pierced in a pattern of overlapping scales. The base is also pierced and the basket stands on an openwork rim foot.

29. Cup and cover. 1705.

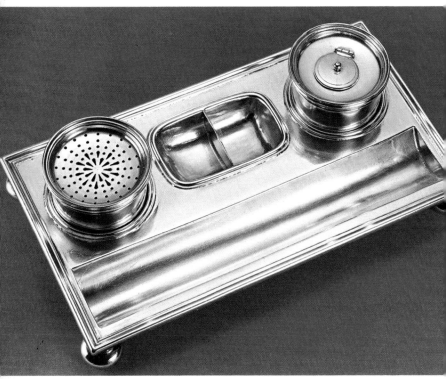

30. Inkstand. *c.* 1705. Length 10½ in, width 5¼ in. Private
collection.

31. Table basket. 1711. Victoria and Albert Museum, London.

midst, and with everywhere a taste for French furniture and fashions, it was not surprising that the silversmiths should also turn to France for inspiration.

THE ENGLISH ROCOCO

The return to sterling silver in 1720 had no appreciable effect on style. There was, indeed, no reason why it should have done, and the plain, often undecorated styles usually associated with the reigns of Queen Anne and George I continued alongside the more elaborate French-influenced Régence designs in demand for more expensive silverwares.

Within a decade, however, the trend towards more ornamental plate had been established. It was undoubtedly the result, not of the return of the slightly harder sterling silver, but of changing taste. Most generations like to have things in a different style from those of their fathers and grandfathers. The cycle of silver design was once again moving towards greater elaboration. In silver these changes seem to appear at about twenty-year intervals. This is perhaps due to the long apprenticeship served to the trade. The silversmith first learns the techniques and makes the patterns chosen by his master. When he himself, after working some ten or fifteen years for another, is his own master, he naturally develops his own style, and is able to offer his patrons silver in the latest manner, just as his contemporaries among the artists and craftsmen—painters, cabinetmakers and potters—also contribute to the development of design.

The change from the formalised Régence motifs of the first quarter of the 18th century to the highly ornamental Rococo style was no rapid one. Gradually, what had been simple and symmetrical became more complicated. Nobility replaced formality, and the baluster curve was twisted into the sinuous fantasy of the Rococo. Indeed, the baluster form still dominated silver styles, even at the height of the Rococo period when it almost vanished beneath a seemingly formless riot of ornamentation. The dictum 'Nature abhors a straight line' was scrupulously observed.

The Rococo, with its roughened surfaces and rocky crags, its shells and scrolls, leaping dolphins and other marine motifs, its naturalistic foliage and flowers, was an echo of the vogue for Romanticism that was to find expression in all the arts. It gave birth to the Romantic novel and the landscaped garden, the strange 'Gothick' of Strawberry Hill and the vogue for grottoes and ruins, to the fashionable occupations of lustrework and shellwork, and the study of flowers and birds, butterflies and trees undertaken by the lady of busy leisure.

To express the Rococo in silver needed superb craftsmanship. Fortunately the leaders of the new style were eminent silversmiths, trained in the formal skills of Régence ornament, and well able to control the curves and fantasies demanded by the new style. They understood that, even amid the decoration, jugs should pour well, salvers and waiters be properly balanced, sauceboats be steady and tea kettles be sturdy enough not to spill scalding water on the mistress of the tea table. Probably because of this practical approach, English Rococo silver rarely reached such extraordinary heights of fantasy as that influenced by Meissonier in France.

Alongside the swirling Rococo motifs there was the more formal late Baroque introduced by Lord Burlington and his protégé William Kent. The Italian

32.   Sugar bowl, teapot and cream jug. 1718, 1713 and 1723. Ashmolean Museum, Oxford. By the end of Queen Anne's reign tea table silver was an important part of the silversmith's production. Both sugar and cream were taken with tea about this period. Sugar bowls were usually quite small and plain, and had small covers. This bowl by William Fleming stands 3 in. high. Teapots were also small and, until the early Rococo period, were usually pear-shaped. This octagonal pot by Humphrey Payne, with straight tapered spout, is engraved with a coat-of-arms in a Baroque cartouche. The small baluster cream jug, 3 in. high, was made by Starling Wilford.

33.   Ewer and basin. 1715. Diameter 11 in. Private collection. The helmet-shaped ewer and basin for rosewater remained important items of plate well into the 18th century. Most were the work of Huguenot silversmiths, but these ones in fact are the work of Edmund Pearce and show the English Baroque treatment of the otherwise French-style ewer. The foot is gadrooned and the base swirl-fluted below a band of simple punched decoration. The shaped rim and the flying scroll

32.

handle are, however, typically Huguenot in inspiration. The deep bowl has a gadrooned rim.

34.   Chocolate pot. 1715. Height 8½ in. S. J. Phillips Ltd, London. This side-handled chocolate pot has a swan-neck spout and plain high-domed cover. The baluster finial covers an aperture in the cover through which the stirring rod was inserted. The pot is quite plain except for a contemporary engraved coat-of-arms in a foliate and scrolling Baroque cartouche. It was made by Nathaniel Locke.

35.   Salt and pepper caster. 1718 and 1723. S. J. Phillips Ltd, London. Early 18th-century small salts were frequently made in sets of two, four or eight. The finest ones were cast and the most popular shape was the octagonal with incurved sides and an oval well for the salt. This salt, from a set of four, was made by Samuel Margas. Early pepper casters were frequently of straight-sided dredger type, known as kitchen peppers. Again the octagonal form was popular, as in this pepper by John Jones.

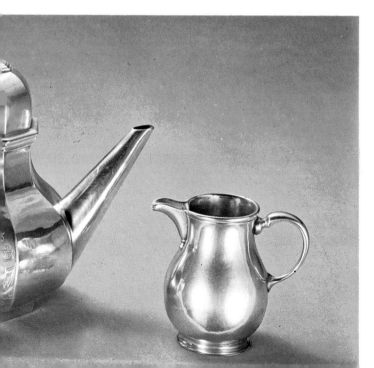

33. Ewer and basin. 1715. Diameter 11 in. Private collection.

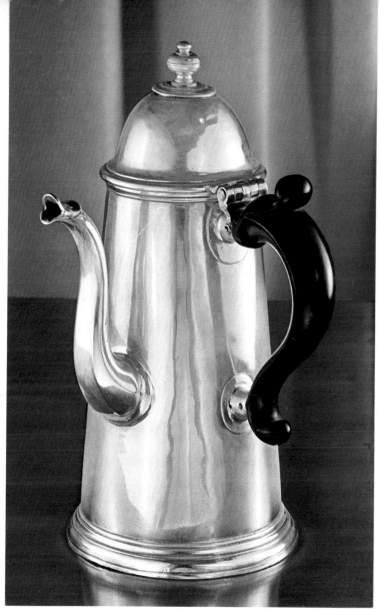

34. Chocolate pot. 1715. Height 8½ in. S. J. Phillips Ltd,
London.

35. Salt and pepper caster. 1718 and 1723. S. J. Phillips Ltd, London.

motifs—lion masks, scrolls, palmers' shells—remained a lasting feature throughout the Rococo period, so that patrons had a choice of decorative styles. By the time George II came to the throne in 1727, few pieces of silver were left uninfluenced by one or other of the new tastes for decoration.

The silversmiths of the period were extremely versatile. They were equally masters of the most complicated Rococo patterns or they could please the eye with the grace and dignity of Palladianism. Sometimes they intermixed the two so that elegant lion and other masks were used in conjunction with the marine motifs of the Rococo, or the asymmetrical 'rockinesses' of the Rococo lightened the severe lines of a simple pot or dish.

The Huguenot immigrants and their descendants, with a long tradition of attention to ornamental detail, proved themselves exceptionally skilled in the new styles—Paul de Lamerie, David Willaume junior, Peter Archambo, Simon Pantin, Paul Crespin, to name but a few. And the English silversmiths had recovered their old skills, so that many fine craftsmen —the Godfreys and the Cafes, George Wickes and Edward Wakelin, John White and Robert Abercromby—vied with them for the still increasing orders for plate that filled their order books. By now it was no longer a simple matter to differentiate between the work of a Huguenot and a London-born silversmith: the continentals had become part of the English scene, and the English looked to France and Italy for new inspiration.

England was wealthy, bridging the transition from a small primarily agricultural country to a great industrial nation. London was a hub of society, but it was a society based still on their country estates which each succeeding generation sought to enlarge, modernise and improve as fashion dictated and finances permitted. London and the spas provided lavish entertainment during the season. There were balls and formal receptions, card parties and tea parties, punch drinking bouts for the men and music and conversation for the women, dinner parties, grand or intimate, and even breakfast parties.

In all this extravagance, the silversmith found plenty of customers, for display pieces and for domestic silver both large and small. Among the former there were still occasionally ewers and basins, great chargers, cups and covers and the salvers made from seals of office. The swirling motifs of the Rococo turned formal palm and acanthus foliage into twisting fronds, made to contrast even more by the use of a matted ground. The two scroll handles were capped with foliage and further enriched with chasing, while the domed cover, also applied with strapwork, was given a bold finial. Probably, too, every inch of the upper part of the body would be flat-chased with scalework and shells above and below the owner's coat-of-arms which was, of course, itself contained in a Rococo, often asymmetrical, cartouche.

By the mid 1740s masks, clusters of fruit, scrolling foliage and even more curved shapes for the body typified the Rococo cup and cover. A fine example of the English Rococo, made for the Goldsmiths' Company by Thomas Farren in 1740, even has different terms on each of the handles—a satyr's head on one, and a Bacchante on the other.

Not all the cups and covers of the Rococo period were, however, in the Rococo style, and side by side with it there was still a steady demand for decorative silver in the more formal Baroque or Palladian manner. But even though it was less gaudy, the silver was nonetheless rich and decorative.

Ministers of the Crown had, from the 16th century onwards, been allowed to keep the silver matrix of the Great Seal or other seal of office when it was made obsolete by the death of the sovereign. They usually had the silver made into commemorative cups, but by the 18th century this more often took the form of large salvers. One of the most famous engravers to work on them was William Hogarth, who in his youth had been apprenticed to the silversmith Ellis Gamble, though later he left the trade in pursuit of his own more profitable kind of engraving. But he has been credited with several exceptional pieces of silver engraving, especially for Paul de Lamerie, and a long tradition, dating back to the 18th century, attributes to him the engraving on the Walpole salver, made from the second Great Seal of Sir Robert Walpole in 1728. Made by Lamerie, it is now in the Victoria and Albert Museum. Another excellent engraver was Simon Gribelin, a Huguenot who had also been apprenticed to a silversmith, and whose known works include a Seal salver engraved in 1702 and a *Book of Ornaments usefull to all Artists*.

It was not only presentation and commemorative plate, however, that was deserving of lavish skill by silversmith and decorator. The ordinary domestic salver was made in every size from the great oblong salver, usually called a 'tea table' in contemporary accounts, to tiny pairs of waiters, perhaps only 5 or 6 inches in diameter. The salvers that in the reign of Queen Anne and George I had often been quite plain, relieved only by a moulded rim and perhaps an engraved coat-of-arms, were by George II's reign often enriched with a Bath or 'pie-crust' border, or with in-

36. Coffee pot. 1723. Height 9½ in. Harvey and Gore, London.

37. Part of a toilet set. 1724. Ashmolean Museum, Oxford.

36.   Coffee pot. 1723. Height 9½ in. Harvey and Gore, London. The tapering straight-sided coffee pot was made throughout the first quarter of the 18th century. Most were plain, and this simple pot with straight octagonal tapering spout, wood handle and domed cover with baluster finial was made by Augustine Courtauld.

37.   Part of a toilet set. 1724. Ashmolean Museum, Oxford. The ewer, snuffers and tray, candlestick, circular casket and small waiter are from the 28-piece toilet set by Paul de Lamerie, made for the Rt Hon. George Treby, M.P., who presented it to his wife on the occasion of their wedding. Lamerie's bill—for £377 13s 10d for making the 'fyne sett of dressing plate', engraving it and supplying the linings, locks for the caskets and so on, the mirror and the brushes and combs—is still extant. The decoration is engraved and flat-chased with shells and strapwork typical of Lamerie's exquisite workmanship.

38.

38.   Sauceboat and a pair of salts. 1725 and 1726-1728. Ash-molean Museum, Oxford. The oval sauce boat, with a lip at either end and scroll side handles, made its appearance about 1715. This fine large example has a wavy moulded rim and is one of a pair made by Nathaniel Gulliver. About 1725 the pedestal salt on a moulded circular foot began to replace the traditional octagonal or circular type. This pair, from a set of four made in 1726-1728 by Anne Tanqueray, has applied formal leafage round the base of the bodies and on the stepped foot. The bowls are gilt inside, and each salt weighs approx-imately $7\frac{1}{2}$ oz.

39.   Wine cooler. 1727. S. J. Phillips Ltd, London. One of a pair of superb Régence style wine coolers made by Thomas Farrer. The bell-shaped body, in the manner of contemporary cups, is decorated with alternate palm leaves and strapwork within shaped surrounds applied on a matted ground. Below the everted gadrooned rim is a band of chased scrolls and strap-work. The central plain section is engraved with a contemporary coat-of-arms.

39. Wine cooler. 1727. S. J. Phillips Ltd, London.

curved corners. For the lover of the new Rococo, even they were too plain, and cast and chased shells, scrolls and guilloche borders were applied to salvers. By 1750, pierced and chased ornament in the Chinese manner had come into fashion, while the surface of the salver was often enriched with flat chasing of the richest sort.

Akin to the design of salvers was that of the standish, or inkstand, though for practical purposes these were often relatively plain. Few inkstands were as elaborate as the one (Plate 47) made for the Goldsmiths' Company by Paul de Lamerie in 1740, and even at the height of the Rococo period William Cripps, George Methuen, John Jacobs and de Lamerie himself were content to be practical, with gadrooning, piercing and shell or scroll feet setting off plain surfaces. The Rococo then only obtruded itself in the decorative pierced tops for the pots, and the intricate cast feet at the corners.

The cast baluster candlestick and its miniature version, the taperstick, remained the basic form. But now the base was usually shaped, with stepped fluting rising to the central well from which the baluster rose, and the fluting was repeated on a large knop below the sconce. In more elaborate versions the base would be overlaid with chased shells and scrollwork, and the stem would swell outwards to the shoulder, the four panels so formed being enriched with scrolls and scalework. Some of the most beautiful of these candlesticks came from the workshops of Eliza Godfrey. French influence was even more pronounced on rare occasions, as in a set of four *rocaille* candlesticks of 1740 by Ann Craig and John Neville, in the style of Meissonier. James Shruder was another silversmith whose candlesticks and candelabra were often in the more extreme Rococo styles, with caryatid and other figure stems that were far more ornate than the everyday products of the specialist candlestick makers such as William Gould, William and John Cafe and William Cripps, though all these found that shaped moulded bases enriched with shells and scrolls, flowers and foliage were almost as much in demand as their more formal sticks on shaped square bases, merely chased with shells at the corners and at the knops above the fluted baluster stems.

Tea table silver, which perhaps remained simple longer than most other silverwares, likewise fell under the spell of the Rococo by the 1740s. In the 1720s the plain pear-shaped pot had become the rounded 'bullet' or globular style, a band of flat-chased ornament at the junction of body and cover often providing the only ornament. But about 1735 the taste for more decorative silver suggested the inverted pear shape, broad at the shoulder and narrowing towards the foot. The spout was curved, often fluted and usually embellished with chasing and applied scrollwork. The kettle likewise followed the new richness, and encrusted ornament, Rococo cartouches in high relief, shells, flowers, grotesque bird-like spouts and ornate scroll supports for the lamp became the order of the day.

Often several kinds of tea were blended by the mistress of the tea table, and canisters to contain the still expensive leaf were a necessary part of the equipment. Now and again the engraved labels 'green' and 'bohea' are found on tea caddies of the period, while a third caddy was sometimes used for sugar. The simple undecorated rectangular caddies by the 1730s generally became round-shouldered and vase-shaped. The domed cover over the hole at the top was enlarged so that a sliding base for filling the canister was no longer necessary.

The vase-shaped caddy of the 1740s, often in the bulging curved form known as *bombé,* was nearly always richly chased with flowers, sprays of foliage and Rococo cartouches for crest or armorials. Sets of three were usual, and most caddy sets were provided with a 'wainscot' case—itself often enriched with silver mounts and inlaid work—in which to lock away the precious tea.

The oriental origin of the beverage and the love of fantasy naturally revived a fashion for *chinoiseries*—at this period repoussé chased, not engraved or flat-chased as in the 1680s. Among the most notable caddies in this style are those of 1747 in the Goldsmiths' Company collection. Made by Paul de Lamerie, they are chased with harvesting scenes, thatched huts and strange trees, with the finials, more accurate than the oriental scenes, representing tea plants. The taste for *chinoiseries* continued well into the formal Neo-classical period in the 1770s.

Although teapot and kettle, caddy and sugar bowl, jugs for milk and cream and a large tea table or salver were all needed for the tea things, few matching services were in fact made. There is a rare set of 1712, comprising teapot, hot water jug and sugar bowl, and another of 1719 with teapot, kettle and coffee pot *en suite,* but it was not until about 1759 or 1760 that the tea service really came into its own—and even then it is rare. Milk or cream jugs and sugar bowls were, on the other hand, often made to match. The small baluster jug was still sometimes made plain, but its popularity was rivalled by the helmet-shaped jug on three feet, with a flying scroll handle. By the end of the Rococo period, these were usually a mass of flower

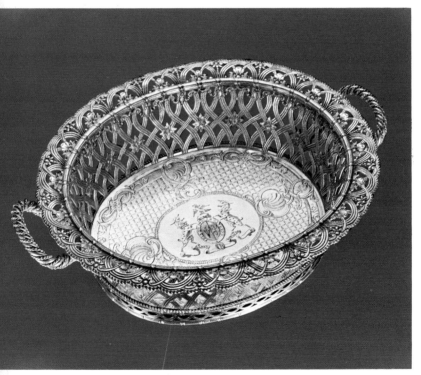

40. Cake basket. 1731. Length 12½ in. Ashmolean Museum, Oxford.

41. Cruet. 1732. S. J. Phillips Ltd, London.

40.   Cake basket. 1731. Length 12½ in. Ashmolean Museum, Oxford. The latticed sides of this oval cake basket, by the famous silversmith Paul de Lamerie, are decorated with flowerets which are picked out with engraving. The everted openwork rim has a reed-and-tie moulding at the junction of the body and rope pattern end handles. The base is engraved with diapers within strapwork of scrolls, shells and foliage around the coat-of-arms of Paulet impaling Tufton.

41.   Cruet. 1732. S. J. Phillips Ltd, London. The ring frame for casters and for oil and vinegar bottles is generally known as a Warwick cruet. Made by Anthony Nelme, this fine cruet on cast scroll supports has a central ring handle and holds a set of three octagonal baluster casters. The largest of the three casters was used for sugar, the smaller probably for pepper, while the third, which shows similar scroll and diaper decoration on the cover, was not pierced and would have been used for dry mustard. A small oval plaque fixed to the front of the frame is engraved with the owner's arms, which also appear on each of the casters.

42.   Pair of jugs. 1732. Height 9¾ in. Ashmolean Museum, Oxford. The baluster-shaped bodies of these jugs by Paul Crespin, a silversmith of Huguenot descent, are applied with alternate plain and intricate straps, with medallions showing male and female heads above scroll and diaper ornament. Foliate and shell chasing decorates the domed cover and the moulded foot of each jug.

43.   Pair of candlesticks. 1737. Height 10 in. The Worshipful Company of Goldsmiths, London. The early Rococo in England added ornament to the basic baluster forms without contorting them. This fine pair of silver-gilt octagonal candlesticks, made by George Wickes, has vase-shaped stems to which are applied masks of nymphs and satyrs, strapwork and foliage, all cast and chased in high relief. The bases are applied with asymmetrical Rococo scroll cartouches.

42. Pair of jugs. 1732.

43. Pair of candlesticks. 1737. Height 10 in. The Worshipful Company of Goldsmiths, London.

and foliate chasing—even sometimes covered with embossed and chased country scenes.

The second quarter of the 18th century saw the birth of the complete dinner service. Plates and dishes had, of course, been made in large numbers for the nobility for many decades, but now there was a host of other silver for the dining table—soup tureens, sauceboats, casters and cruets, salts, baskets for bread, cake and fruit, dessert dishes and the grand centre-pieces known as épergnes.

Sometimes the dinner service came into the possession of the great families as 'Indenture Plate'. This was actually issued to ambassadors and other officers of state on their appointment, and was retained by them, in lieu of payment for their services, when they retired from office.

One of the most important items of dining table silver introduced during the early Georgian period was the soup tureen. Often very large, it possibly developed from the two-handled covered bowls of the 17th century and from the individual écuelle. Most tureens were oval, though a few were circular. A central foot or four cast feet raised the hot bowl of the tureen off the table-top, and sturdy side handles permitted carrying it when it was full. The feet and handles of tureens at once provided an opportunity for elaborate decoration, and this tendency persisted even among those patrons who preferred simpler styles than the Rococo.

For the Rococoists, the uses of tureens suggested a whole group of fantasies. Marine motifs were highly popular, with oysters, lobsters, mussels and dolphins curling and nestling against rocky backgrounds. Vegetables, too, were used with aplomb: a particularly fine Rococo tureen made in 1752 by Frederick

Kandler for the Earl of Bristol has a collection of onions, cabbage, celery and artichoke on the cover, themes taken up at this period by the English porcelain makers. Indeed Nicholas Sprimont, manager of the Chelsea factory, was himself a working silversmith from Liège who registered his mark in London in 1742. The high Rococo style was also much employed by his neighbour Paul Crespin, another silversmith of Huguenot descent. In two consecutive years Crespin made tureens that were, in effect, centrepieces. One, in the royal collection, is dated 1741 and consists of an oval tureen supported by dolphins and mermaids. Its predecessor, dated 1740 and now in the Toledo Museum of Art, Ohio, replaces the sea creatures with two figures of recumbent hinds, while the cover is a mass of life-size silver fruit.

Sauceboats, which had been introduced about 1715, were at first plain, with a lip at either end and central scroll handles. Later the boat-shaped version on three legs or with a central moulded oval foot placed the handle at one end, opposite the lip. In the hands of the ornamentalists, the sauceboat indeed became a marine vessel, a cockleshell, perhaps, with tritons or other sea creatures forming the flying scroll handle, and a rocky promontory for the oval foot.

While Voltaire castigated the English for having only one sauce, the same could not be said of their sauceboats. Plain or fanciful, made in pairs or even in sets of four or more, they showed every phase of silver style. The earliest decorative period favoured lion-mask knuckles, shell motifs at the rim, delightful double-scroll handles, sometimes leaf-capped, and flat-chased borders. Shell fluting provided a more decorative style, and then, about 1740, came the most extravagant of all sauceboat designs—the confections

44. Soup tureen. 1739. Height 15½ in. Frank Partridge Ltd,
London.

44.   Soup tureen. 1739. Height 15½ in. Frank Partridge Ltd, London. One of a pair made by John Eckfourd, showing the transition from the Régence to the Rococo style. Beautifully executed strapwork with alternating piercing and applied masks decorate the oval bodies, between the cast boars' head handles.

45.   Two sauceboats. 1742 and 1737. Ashmolean Museum, Oxford. Rococo at its most Rococo—two examples, each from a pair of sauceboats by Charles Kandler. The one with a grotesque eagle handle is chased in high relief with fish, birds and animals surrounded by cartouches of shells and scrolls. The shell-shaped sauceboat is applied with tiny models of snails, ladybirds, crabs and scorpions, while the handle is formed as a stork holding a snake in its bill, rising from a tree-trunk base.

46.   Two-handled cup and cover. 1740. Height 15½ in. The Worshipful Company of Goldsmiths, London. This two-handled cup and cover with long bell-shaped body is superbly decorated in the Rococo manner, with an applied chased figure of Minerva on one side and the arms of the Goldsmiths' Company on the other, surrounded by Rococo scrolls, flowers and vines. The domed cover is also richly applied with scrolls, masks, flowers and foliage, and has a pineapple finial. The asymmetry is further accented by the different handles, one terminating in a satyr's head, the other in a bacchante's. The cup was made in 1740 by Thomas Farren who, the following year, made three more to match for the Goldsmiths' Company.

47.   Inkstand with bell. 1740. Length 16 in. The Worshipful Company of Goldsmiths, London. In 1740 the Goldsmiths' Company had very little early plate. One of its treasures was the small silver-gilt bell presented to them by Sir Robert Vyner in 1666. The Goldsmiths commissioned Paul de Lamerie to make an inkstand to accommodate this bell, and he produced one of the most beautiful and lavish inkstands in existence. It is decorated with asymmetrical scrolls and garlands of flowers and with, at each corner, a mask of Jupiter, Minerva, Mercury and Juno cast in high relief.

48.   Coffee pot. 1745. Victoria and Albert Museum, London. Basically the form of the teapot and the coffee pot changed little during the Rococo period, the decoration merely enhancing the older form. The coffee pot—left plain even at this date as often as it was decorated—was a tapering shape with 'tucked-in' base on a spreading rim foot, and with curved spout fluted at the base. This Rococo version by Robert Innes is chased with scrolls, flowers and scalework, and also has an applied mask at the base of the spout.

45. Two sauceboats. 1742 and 1737.

46. Two-handled cup and cover. 1740. Height 15½ in. The Worshipful Company of Goldsmiths, London.

47. Inkstand with bell. 1740. Length 16 in. The Worshipful
Company of Goldsmiths, London.

48. Coffee pot. 1745. Victoria and Albert Museum, London.

and marine fantasies of de Lamerie, Kandler and Sprimont. The central foot was revived, richly chased, of course, while the handle became distinctly uncomfortable in the form of a curling sea-serpent or even a hovering bird of prey, as on a pair by Kandler in the Ashmolean Museum at Oxford (Plate 45).

Casters for sugar, spice and dry mustard escaped, it seems, the most extravagant forms of the Rococo. The baluster form remained the usual style, perhaps enriched with repoussé chased flowers and scrolls, but for the most part relatively plain, relying for its appeal on the intricately pierced covers.

Pierced work during the age of ornament was of a very high standard. One of the delights of English silver is the table basket. By 1730 the oval swing-handled basket was established, although occasionally one comes across one with the small D-handles that had been favoured in Queen Anne's reign, or with no handle at all. Early Georgian baskets were usually mounted on a low rim foot, sometimes everted and almost always cast and pierced. The sides were often interwoven designs borrowed from wickerwork. The geometrical theme tended to disappear, however, with the advent of the Rococo, and many table baskets featured two, three or even more different patterns of piercing. The foot and chased rim mounts were often enriched with shells, masks and sprays of flowers and fruit, and the swing handles were pierced, engraved or chased.

Baskets and shallow fluted dishes were often suspended on frames or branches to form épergnes, the centrepieces used to pile fruit, sweetmeats and so on at the table. Some épergnes even incorporated candle-holders, and must have looked very lacy and lavish in the flickering candlelight.

Silver drinking vessels, perforce, had to be fairly simple, and even at the height of the Rococo most punch bowls were quite plain. Tankards and mugs tended to follow traditional styles, the plain baluster form introduced in the early Huguenot period continuing to be made. Jugs, too, were usually simple, of baluster form on a sturdy moulded foot and with a bold scroll handle.

For coffee the tapering straight-sided pot gave way to that with a tucked in base, but apart from decorative applied work round the sockets of the wood or ivory handle, and at the base of the faceted spout, few coffee pots were wildly Rococo. Of course marine fantasy did appear from time to time, and there was a brief vogue for the coffee and chocolate pot in the French style on three cast scroll legs. But though flowers and scrolls might make an occasional appearance, the coffee pot, like the mug, was really an everyday piece of silver and carried on the tradition of simple sturdy silver, a tradition that, in fact, continued little changed for less expensive silverwares throughout the age of ornament.

About 1755 even the most ardent Rococoists began to tire of the extravagant and disorderly decoration they had created. Symmetry began to return. Formal borders, lion masks, guilloche mouldings and the geometrical motifs of Chinese Chippendale began to influence silver designs—a return to the grand manner of the Baroque, to gadroons and mouldings, and even to large plain surfaces. The stage was set for the next great style in the history of English silver—the new classicism of Robert Adam.

THE AGE OF ADAM

The rise of Neo-classicism was really inevitable. Within living memory silver and the other applied arts had moved from the severely simple to the grand Baroque, through Rococo and 'the gaudy gout of the Chinese' —even touching on the Gothic Revival. For a dozen or so years at the middle of the century, almost every style had its adherents, but nothing definitive emerged. Then about 1760 the patrons knew again just what they wanted. They wanted classicism.

London society prided itself on its interest in art and architecture. Continental travel was one of the essentials of a good education, and was also a convenient means of acquiring an art collection. When the excavations at Herculaneum, Pompeii and other classical sites were under way, it was also a useful way of acquiring status symbols in the form of Greek and Roman antiquities. Artists and architects also saw their opportunities in the uncovering of ancient ruins, and made detailed and painstaking scale drawings of the finds. The result was a series of elegant publications paid for by subscription by all who could afford to be in the fashion.

In 1753 Wood's *Ruins of Palmyra* made its appearance, followed in 1757 by the companion volume on Baalbek. That year, too, saw the beginning of *Le Antichità di Ercolano,* and in 1762 came Stuart and Revett's *Antiquities of Athens.* Among the most eager and talented of the students who visited the ancient cities was a young Scottish architect called Robert Adam. He not only designed buildings for his clients, but he took a hand in their interior design and furnishings, from ceilings and doors to carpets, furniture and silver. In the 1760s such meddling in other men's crafts was perhaps less disastrous than it became half a century later, when men trained in one medium foisted their designs indiscriminately and inappropriately on others.

The Neo-classical approach to antiquity was not bound by any hard and fast rules. The aim was simply to draw upon 'the most elegant ornaments of the most refined Grecian articles'. The fact that many were Roman did not trouble the Neo-classicists at all. For the silversmith the vase and the urn were readily adaptable shapes. Decoratively laurel festoons, anthemion or honeysuckle motifs and Vitruvian scrolls were a pleasantly formal relief after the contortions of the Rococo. Engraving, little used except for armorials in the Rococo period, was revived, and a new and very positive method, called bright-cut engraving, contributed to the lightness and delicacy of the Adam style.

The period of the new classicism was also the dawning of a new age—the age of the machine. The fact that various crafts were imitated by machines caused little or no alarm at the time. People were far more excited by the importance of inventions that would help to make more and sell more to an ever expanding market. And the new Adam styles, with the simplicity of line and the restrained ornament of pierced galleries and engraved festoons were highly suited to the newly discovered abilities of the fly-press and the stamping machine.

Two great centres of metalworking sprang up—in Birmingham and Sheffield. Sheffield, since early times a centre of knife making, now also became important for the development of Sheffield plate, a method of fusing a thin layer of silver on to a core of copper, and for the use of stamping silver parts. Candlesticks, in particular, became very much the work of the Sheffield manufacturers, who stamped out the silver in sections and then assembled the parts, filling the bases with resin or other heavy substances to weight them. In Birmingham, too, the plating and stamping industry was growing fast, with one of the leading industrialists of all time, Matthew Boulton, very much to the fore at his Soho works.

The huge quantities of silver made in Birmingham and Sheffield caused much trouble and delay in the assay offices. Everything had to be sent to either London, Chester or Newcastle for assay and marking, and Matthew Boulton and his colleagues set to work to force the authorities to establish assay offices in their thriving cities. Despite bitter opposition from the Goldsmiths' Company, his efforts at last succeeded, and in 1773 both the Sheffield and the Birmingham assay offices were opened. Boulton had won, though it is interesting to find candlesticks and other silver of the period often overstamped with the mark of London makers or retailers. But perhaps it is significant that today, of all the provincial assay offices, only Birmingham and Sheffield survive in England.

The Adam style of Neo-classicism dominated silver design from about 1770 to 1795. The classical urn appeared everywhere for cups and covers, jugs, teapots, tea urns and tureens. Classical columns were a natural inspiration for candlesticks, though the interpreters added especial grace in the use of curved branches for candelabra, which were a far cry from the stateliness of a classical building. Indeed it was often the classical manner rather than imitation that marked the silver of the period. Pierced galleries, achieved by a new tool for the silversmith, the piercing saw, were

49. Inkstand. 1745. Length 10¾ in. Private collection.

50. Tea kettle. 1753. Victoria and Albert Museum, London

49.   Inkstand. 1745. Length 10¾ in. Private collection. Even at the height of the Rococo period inkstands were often quite simple. This oblong inkstand, made by Robert Innes, stands on four foliate feet and has a gadrooned and shell-mounted rim. The inkwell, pounce-pot and bell fit over circular depressions in the stand, and there is a shallow trough for the pens.

50.   Tea kettle. 1753. Victoria and Albert Museum, London. The tea kettle was an essential part of the hostess's drawing-room equipment, and from Queen Anne's time onwards, kettles were made with elegant scroll-supported lamps. During the Rococo period pierced and chased aprons concealed the lamp, while the kettle itself was an inverted pear-shape enriched with scrolls, flowers, shells and foliage chased in high relief. This fine example was made by William Grundy.

51.   Tea caddy. 1756. Victoria and Albert Museum, London. Circular *bombé* tea caddy by Herbert and Co., decorated with swirl-flutes and trails of flowers, with Rococo scrolls and shells between and a flower finial. The style of the chasing much appealed to the decorators of the early 19th century who ornamented much earlier plain silver with such neo-Rococo work.

52.   Set of four candlesticks. 1762. Carrington and Co. Ltd, London. This set of four cast candlesticks, on shaped bases decorated with scrolls and shells, are typical of the late Rococo in England. They were made by Ebenezer Coker.

51. Tea caddy. 1756. Victoria and Albert Museum, London.

52. Set of four candlesticks. 1762. Carrington and Co. Ltd, London.

much used for all kinds of baskets, centrepieces and for salts and mustard pots. These were provided with blue glass liners, which were a most pleasing contrast with the grey lustre of the silver, and emphasised the lightness and grace of the designs.

The formal charm of the Adam Neo-classicism was also most successfully brought out by the use of engraved motifs. Borders of husks, lotus flowers, honeysuckle—or anthemion—rosettes, palmettes, scrolls, reeding, ribbonwork and other formal themes were picked out in the incisive brilliance of bright-cut engraving. Even today, many bright-cut pieces remain brilliant, though sometimes long wear has dimmed the sharpness of the cut.

Applied decoration was not, however, banished, and many typical Adam wares were enriched with applied palm leaf and festoon motifs, or even richly embossed in low relief. Beading, done with a small punch and used with considerable accuracy, was a popular decoration for edge mounts, and so was reed-and-tie and plain reeding. Fluting was, of course, revived to interpret the flutes of classical columns, and small applied medallions showing usually classical heads or themes, though sometimes adapted for English scenes, also became fashionable. Among modellers who, it seems, prepared moulds for silversmiths, potters and cabinetmakers, was James Tassie, a gemcutter, and his silversmith customers including his neighbours, Fogelburg and Gilbert, who were foremost in their use of miniature applied medallions on silver.

The geometrical pierced galleries used by Chippendale in his 'Chinese' furniture had little direct effect on silver designs, but there was a definite *chinoiserie* revival in silver during the late 1770s. In fact there was almost a rebellion against classicism while still bowing to it with formality, as in the delightful square tea chest caddies which followed the design of the plain chests in which tea was imported, and which were usually topped with charming Chinaman or teaplant finials. One caddy, now in the Victoria and Albert Museum, even adds a Greek key pattern border and a husk and ribbon oval cartouche for the owner's crest—very much in the Adam manner, at which the makers, George Cowles and Louisa Courtauld, always excelled.

The impact of Adam Neo-classicism swept through everything. Whether a piece was of silver or of Sheffield plate, richly decorated with applied work and chasing, or plain except for a reeded or beaded border, of heavy gauge silver or flimsy and inexpensive for a wide general market, it followed classical themes in shape as well as in its ornament. Some wares, for which there was of course no precedent in classical times—teapots and sugar baskets, salts and mustard pots, and many other domestic silverwares—had to be based only derivatively on classical forms. If a piece could not be vase-shaped or urn-shaped, then it was usually based on the oval, and drum-shaped teapots, table salts and other objects adapted themselves to Neo-classicism. But where form could not be strictly classical the inspiration for the decoration could, and the classical theme permeated everything.

In its most expensive forms, silver still remained predominantly decorative, rich, still sometimes gilt, and seldom dully repetitive. The silver gilt toilet service by two of the best London makers, Daniel Smith and Robert Sharp, now in the Kungl. Livrustkammaren in Stockholm, shows the richness of the Adam style at its best. The oval boxes are enriched with ap-

53. Teapot. 1763. Victoria and Albert Museum, London.

53.   Teapot. 1763. Victoria and Albert Museum, London. The inverted pear-shape for the teapots allowed the silversmith to lavish decoration on the broad shoulders. In this pot, by William and James Priest, swirling scrolls and foliage cover the body, surrounding the asymmetrical cartouche for the owner's crest. The swan-neck spout is fluted and chased with foliage, while a flower and leaf knop forms the finial.

54.   Three tea caddies. 1778, 1769 and 1765. Private collection. *Chinoiserie* themes were a natural decorative style for tea caddies during the 1760s and 1770s. In the one on the right the *bombé* shape, favoured during the late Rococo period, is chased overall with Chinese figures amid Rococo scrolls and flowers. On one side a Chinaman is playing a mandolin beneath an umbrella, while on the other a Chinese figure holds a basket of fruit. The ends show temples, and the finial on the cover is formed as a reclining Chinese coolie. The caddy is 15 cm. high, and was made by Pierre Gillois. The rectangular style of tea caddy was popular from about 1730 until the 1770s. This Rococo caddy (left) follows the style of the earlier Rococo caddies of Lamerie and Crespin. Shells and scrolls are chased in high relief on the sides, while a Rococo panel on either side shows a Chinaman picking tea. The sliding cover has a realistically modelled finial in the form of two flowers. A number of caddies were made in imitation of the chests in which the tea was imported. In the centre the square caddy with hinged cover, by Aaron Le Sturgeon, is a later version of the tea-chest caddy. The sides are bright-cut, with festoons of flowers and ribbon motifs between foliage borders. A chased and fluted urn finial shows the Adam influence.

55.   Mustard pot, pepper caster and double salt. Length of salt $4\frac{1}{2}$ in. S. J. Phillips Ltd, London. Typical condiment pots of the 1760s. The drum-shaped mustard pot is delightfully pierced with birds, foliage and flowers between vertical bars. The engraving on the cover echoes the flower motif and the slender double-scroll handle is leaf-capped. It is dated 1768. The simple baluster caster with a flame finial also shows the later Rococo fashion of flower piercing. It was made in 1769 by John Delmester, who specialised in casters. The double basket salts, with their intertwined rope handles, show an early use of classical Vitruvian scrolls.

56.   Candlestick. 1767. Victoria and Albert Museum, London.
Like the great majority of English silverware, candlesticks were
not basically much changed during the Rococo period, though
decorative motifs might mean some asymmetry of form. This
candlestick by Ebenezer Coker shows the application of
Rococo scrolls and foliage to elaborate an otherwise simply
designed tall baluster candlestick.

54.   Three tea caddies. 1778, 1769 and 1765.

55. Mustard pot, pepper caster and double salt. Length of salt 4½ in. S. J. Phillips Ltd, London.

56. Candlestick. 1767. Victoria and Albert Museum, London.

plied festoons and medallions—perhaps by Tassie—
and their covers are repoussé chased with palm leaves.
The formal yet beautifully executed Vitruvian scrolls
on a matted ground, the palm leaves, rosettes and husk
festoons found in many an Adam drawing were interpreted by the leading silversmiths of the 1770s and
1780s, and they appeared on a huge number of fine and
heavy tureens, sauce tureens (the sauceboat vanished
almost entirely in favour of the lidded tureen during
the Adam period), candlesticks, candelabra, jugs and
teapots, coffee pots and urns, and of course on the
grand cups and covers made for race trophies.

But there was a large market for less expensive
wares. Sheffield plate found its place in many homes,
but there were still many who preferred inexpensive
silver, however thin the gauge and scanty the decoration, to the new silver on copper. Candlesticks, loaded
to give them stability but in fact really sheaths of
silver over a lead or resin core, jugs and pots on rim
pedestal stands and with slender loop handles and not
very sturdy bodies, salts and baskets made up from
mass-manufactured parts all helped to supply this
demand.

Decoration for this 'middle class' silver was naturally fairly simple. A few engraved lines would repro-
duce the grand formal festoons and classical medallions on the more expensive entirely hand-worked
and hand-raised pieces made for the wealthy. Not that
all of this type of silver was of poor quality, flimsily
made and sketchily decorated. Much was well made,
sturdy and though fairly simple (because in silver
good decoration has always been expensive) it was
well executed. The rise of the specialist makers—a
trend that had been growing since the early part of the
century—meant at least some consistency in standards.

Most salts were the work of the Hennell family, casters were made by the Daniels among others, and the Batemans, while often making special orders of exceptional quality, also created tea table wares, baskets, salts and casters for this large new 'middle class' market. Once away from the leaders of silver fashion—from the splendid shops of Rundell and Bridge on Ludgate Hill, and of Wakelin and Taylor, later Wakelin and Garrard, in the West End of London, for instance— the Neo-classical style was a very watered down version of the original Adam.

By the end of the century taste was once more turning full circle. Walpole had long before castigated Adam designs as 'sippets of embroidery'. Even the King was heard to pronounce that 'the Adams have introduced too much of neatness and prettiness'. His son did more than simply comment. He gave a lead and sponsored the grand style that has become known as Regency—though in fact the Regency style made its impact at least ten years before Prince George became the Regent.

REGENCY AND AFTER

It is difficult to say just when the style known as Regency came into being. It certainly overlapped the actual Regency period, which only lasted from 1811 to 1820, and it is probably truer to regard it as including the era of the Prince Regent's influence on taste from about 1795 until his death in 1830. The early Regency style was a natural outcome of Neo-classicism as practised by the Adam brothers. Its importance was accentuated by 'Prinny'—George, Prince of Wales, 'the most accomplished man of his age'.

He had been born in 1770, and by the time he was twenty, the Prince had established himself in London society as a leader of taste and a critical enthusiast. 'Prinny' was the last of the great dilettanti. He was certainly a man of taste, even of genius, although sometimes these qualities were thwarted or mistimed. He was as elegant and debonair as he was at times wanton and selfish. He could be gross and self-indulgent, or he could be sensitive and immediately and brilliantly appreciative of the arts.

During a visit to Weymouth, his father the King had been introduced to a farmer called Bridge, whose cousin was the partner of Philip Rundell, goldsmith and jeweller on Ludgate Hill in London. On his return, George III began to patronise the firm of Rundell and Bridge, and soon, 'whenever he heard of a Marriage about to take place in the Great World, he would almost command the parties to go to Ludgate Hill for any Plate or Jewels they might want for the occasion, and very many splendid orders were received in consequence'. So wrote one of Rundell's employees, George Fox, in his memoirs of the company written in 1846.

Naturally Rundell and Bridge quickly assumed a leading rôle among the London silversmiths. They were appointed to the Prince of Wales. They were an ambitious firm, and saw their opportunities in the lavish patronage of the court. But if they set their sights high, their standards were also high. In Paul Storr, for instance, they found a master silversmith whose work was virtually faultless and who could carry out the immense tasks set for him by the sculptor-designers such as Flaxman whom Rundell's employed. For it is modelling and chased enrichments that typify the Regency style, boldness and

57. Candlestick. 1771. Victoria and Albert Museum, London.

58. Cake basket. 1771. Victoria and Albert Museum, London.

59. Coffee pot. 1774. Carrington and Co. Ltd, London.

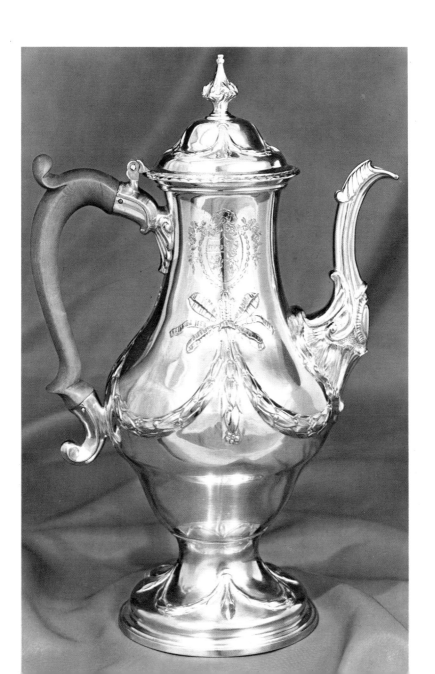

57.   Candlestick. 1771. Victoria and Albert Museum, London.
John Carter made this richly chased square-based candlestick
in 1771. Bold flowers ornament each corner of the gadrooned
base, while the baluster stem is chased with caryatid figures in
the four panels. But about the same time, Carter was one of the
leading silversmiths carrying out the really formal designs of
Adam, and one of his classical candlesticks, made in 1767, has
its original in one of Adam's own drawings.

58.   Cake basket. 1771. Victoria and Albert Museum, London.
After the elaborate pierced work of the Rococo period and
before Adam formality made its full impact, many cake baskets
were designed using silver wire overlaid with naturalistic motifs
such as sprays of flowers and ears of wheat. This graceful
basket, with openwork swing handle and pierced foot which
hint at Adam classicism, was made by Richard Mills.

59.   Coffee pot. 1774. Carrington and Co. Ltd, London. By
the late 1760s, the swirling motifs of the Rococo were losing
popularity, but something of the style lingered on well into the
Neo-classical period. This pear-shaped coffee pot by Charles
Wright shows the scrolls and shells of the Rococo on the
swan-necked spout and on the handle sockets, but hints at
classicism with the laurel festoons and pendants applied to the
body and domed cover.

60.   Sugar basket. 1776. Victoria and Albert Museum,
London. Adam formality and classical festoons and palm leaf
motifs for a sugar basket. Blue glass, here scalloped at the top
to follow the line of the basket, was fashionable and most
effectively used for sugar baskets, sweetmeat baskets and
cream pails.

60. Sugar basket. 1776.

depth of decoration that replaced the neat engraved motifs associated with Adam Neo-classicism.

It was mostly still a style of classical inspiration, but a Roman splendour overlaid the slim columns and festoons of the 1780s and 1790s. 'Massiveness', declared C. H. Tatham, the sculptor, is 'the principal characteristic of good Plate'. He enjoined the silversmith to consider 'Chasing . . . as a branch of Sculpture'. No one stopped to consider whether silver was a suitable material for sculpture, or whether sculpture was suited to the dining saloon and the drawing-room.

The silversmiths, pressed primarily by Rundell and Bridge, took up the challenge, and with immense skill created the style that was to be named after the most esteemed of their patrons, the Prince of Wales. But like the Prince, whose artistic temperament changed as often as the weathervane, the Regency style was an ever changing pattern. Within twenty years, it ran through a whole octave of styles—Greek, Roman, Egyptian, Middle Eastern, spiced with a dash of *chinoiserie*, varied with Romanticism, and freely mixed with a revival of Baroque and an almost exact imitation of the Rococo.

It could be said that the Regency style of silver was a development of all that had gone before. Basic forms were usually of classical origin, even to the extent of being exact copies of the antique—as Theed's carefully measured drawings of the Warwick vase, a marble frequently copied in silver by Paul Storr and, in the 1820s, when Storr had left Rundell's, by Philip Rundell. This was not a trait peculiar to the silversmiths, either: Wedgwood, for instance, made innumerable copies of the Portland vase and of other classical pots. But many of the items in the silversmiths' repertoire had no classical originals, and neither designer nor maker nor patron seemed much troubled by the fact that shape and ornament mixed one style with another.

The long Napoleonic wars had, strangely, several important contributions to make to silversmithing. A piece of plate was considered a highly suitable reward for deserving officers of the army or the navy. Indeed, from the end of the American civil war until Waterloo, the years were studded with memorable—and therefore commemorative—events. The most notable was Trafalgar in 1805, and after this naval commanders were awarded silver vases, most of them made by Benjamin Smith (for Rundell's, of course) to a design by Flaxman. They varied in size and value, according to the rank of the recipient, the two largest being reserved for Lady Nelson, and for Lord Nelson, brother of the Admiral.

The war, too, created a vast new market for silverwares. 'The Nobility and Gentry,' wrote Fox in his memoirs, 'seemed anxious to vie with each other in every species of luxury and extravagance.' Only the poor suffered from the war. Landlords kept rents soaring, manufacturers of supplies grew rich overnight, though the sudden vagaries of the market wrought havoc with many merchants unable to keep pace or unprepared for change. But hundreds succeeded in amassing fortunes with their factories and by trade with countries all over the world. For any family which considered itself in the least refined, a show of silver was as essential as the tea and talk that played its part in the duchess's drawing-room and the shopkeeper's parlour alike.

Factory production proved a boon to those catering for the growing middle class market. Machines, far from being deplored, were welcomed as a means of producing quantities of goods at an economic price. The workshops could turn out parts by the hundred—teapot bodies and tankard bodies, handles and spouts, feet and finials, ready pierced galleries for salts and small baskets, sections of candlesticks, and so on. Openwork patterns could be cut in the fly-press in a fraction of the time that it took to hand-pierce them. There was, of course, a certain loss of quality, but that did not unduly disturb the buyer whose chief concern was plenty of silverware at a moderate price. It was enough to be told that a piece was in the fashion.

It did not take long for the silversmiths in the busy new factories in Sheffield and Birmingham to emulate the designs that the London firms were commissioning. Often the only difference is discernible in the actual craftsmanship. The London trade, then as now, was less reliant on mechanical aids than that in Birmingham or Sheffield, but even London silversmiths sometimes overstamped their mark on Sheffield-made candlesticks—proof indeed that they considered them of suitable quality to put to sale under their name.

While Rundell, Bridge and Rundell (as the firm was styled from 1806 onwards) were concentrating on spectacular silver, not all the fashionable world obeyed the King and purchased their gold and silver there. In the West End, Wakelin and Garrard, later to be appointed crown jewellers, continued to supply a large number of the nobility with fine plate—though they too followed the trend towards more splendid silver. And further away from the fashion of Bond Street and Pall Mall, the Haymarket and Piccadilly, smaller firms such as Hester Bateman's successors, Peter, Anne and William Bateman, were making good silver for less lavishly minded customers.

The tea service was equally important in the man-

61. Soup tureen. 1777. Length 13¾ in. Private collection.

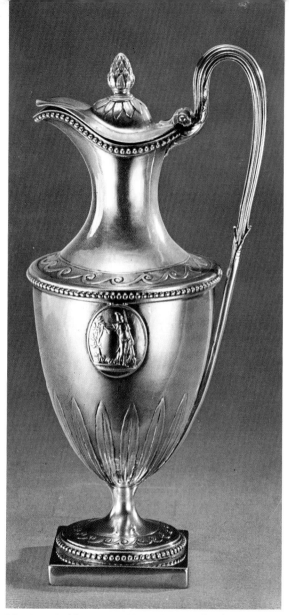

62. Jug. 1780. Height 7 in. Private collection.

63. Gravy pot and two sauce tureens. 1785. Private collection.

61.   Soup tureen. 1777. Length 13¾ in. Private collection. This large soup tureen, made by Daniel Smith and Robert Sharp, shows all the ingredients of Adam Neo-classicism at its best, with superbly chased palm leaf decoration, applied festoons and beading, anthemion scrolls, rosettes and, on either side, an oval classical medallion.

62.   Jug. 1780. Height 7 in. Private collection. This small vase-shaped jug in the Neo-classical style stands on a square plinth base, which rises to a circular foot with beaded and Vitruvian scroll decoration. The same motifs are repeated on the shoulders, above the palm leaf chased body. The latter is applied on either side with an oval medallion, probably by Tassie, who specialised in classical medallions and gems and who worked near Andrew Fogelburg and Stephen Gilbert, the makers of the jug.

63.   Gravy pot and two sauce tureens. 1785. Private collection. Two sauce tureens from a set of four and an argyle, or gravy pot, made by Carter, Smith and Sharp. The graceful tureens and the helmet shaped argyle are half-fluted and the edges are gadrooned. Each stand, tureen and cover is numbered and fits only its partner perfectly.

64.   Épergne. 1790. Garrard and Co. Ltd, London. Basket centrepieces, known as épergnes, were fashionable for holding fruit and sweetmeats, especially during the second half of the 18th century. About 1775 the Rococo style gave way to the Adam Neo-classical. The circular dishes became boat-shaped baskets, and the foliate stands and branches were transformed into slender frames with reeded supports and husk festoons. This épergne, which has a large oval centre basket pierced and chased with bat's-wing fluting, is surrounded by eight smaller dishes and was made by William Pitts.

64. Epergne. 1790.

sion or in the little villas that were springing up in the suburbs. The flat-based oval drum teapot of the Adam period survived well into the 1800s, but it often carried half-fluting instead of engraving. Gradually, however, the urn-shape, which was still favoured for coffee pots and hot water jugs, began to dictate the style of the teapot, which was made with a rim foot, or even a high spreading foot that even obviated the need for a teapot stand. The body of the pot became squatter and more rounded, with a wide rim round the lid that stood away from the body like a collar. At first spouts were long and with slender curves, but soon they were superseded by short, rather broad-based ones. Tea services were, of course, the rule, so that sugar bowl and milk jug were designed *en suite*, with bulging bodies and large loop handles that set the style for the remainder of the 19th century. The pierced basket for sugar and the cream pail with its blue glass liner vanished from the tea table as surely as the plain surface of silver vanished beneath a mass of chasing.

The decoration of all silver, old and new, was almost a ritual in the years after Waterloo. Silversmiths' ledgers record again and again the addition of chasing to earlier plain silver, a trend that continued, unfortunately, throughout the 19th century and, to the collector's chagrin, has ruined many a fine early 18th-century piece. Flowers and foliage, shells and other motifs, often quite inappropriate to the style of the original, were chased on coffee pots and mugs, casters and milk jugs.

Those who could afford them ordered massive and highly decorated candlesticks and candelabra from the London makers. The fluted vase-shaped and baluster stems of the 1790s were by 1800 enriched with applied foliate borders, and many were also provided with branches, often in Sheffield plate, to transform them into the more fashionable candelabra. One of the most gifted of the London candlestick makers was Benjamin Smith, whose work was largely retailed by Rundell, Bridge and Rundell. Smith managed to create a Regency style that made use of all the fashionable classical motifs—lotus leaves and fan palms, rosettes and guilloche work, acanthus foliage and Egyptian columns, triple caryatid figures and winged sphinxes. Yet his candlesticks rarely overwhelm with their multiplicity of motifs. He managed to harness all the varying themes into an orderly design for rich massive grandeur. Working alone, or with his partner Digby Scott, Smith created most of the designs that a year or two later were repeated by that other master craftsman Paul Storr. On the whole, Benjamin Smith's work relies rather more on classical themes, while Storr tended to excel at the revived Rococo of the period.

Scott, Smith and Storr all worked chiefly for Rundell's, and it must not be thought that they entirely dominated the field. In the West End, William Pitts was also following the new Rococo trend, making massive and richly chased sticks for Wakelin and Garrard, among others. In Sheffield, too, the workshops were busy, striving to emulate the ever changing styles of the Regency and translate them into the fine but much less costly loaded candlesticks in which they specialised.

Changing tastes were perhaps the chief reason for the unsettled styles of English silver from the end of the Adam period until the new youthful revival a century and a half later. A wine cooler might be richly Baroque in 1818, a riot of Rococo a year later.

One year a large waiter might recall the 1750s, the next be transformed into a severely classical oval tray.

The Regency was a great age for the dining table. Some tables must have groaned beneath the weight of silver as well as the great quantities of foods served. Centre-pieces were much in fashion, the many-branched épergne of the 18th century now becoming a grand central stand. It had perhaps only one great dessert dish, often made of cut glass, but in the richest examples of beautifully interwoven silver or silver-gilt wire supported, perhaps, by a trio of graceful caryatid figures in classical robes. Plinths were often triangular, like those of the large standing candelabra, and Paul Storr in particular liked dolphin supports with flower-chased festoons between.

Dessert and cake baskets were often almost entirely of wirework, sometimes plain, sometimes overlaid with trailing vines. Others were distinctly Rococo in inspiration, and there was a fashion for dessert dishes, rather than baskets, with broad cast chased and pierced rims. One late example, made by Benjamin Smith in 1835, has a heavy border of masks, leopards and vases on a vine rim that must have owed its design to the great salver or oval tray made by Philip Rundell in 1822, a superb piece of chasing which could hardly be equalled by any silversmith today.

Vine themes were naturally a suitable ornament for bottle coasters and coolers, and sorted well with the use of classical motifs. The most expensive type of coaster had the vines pierced out, but the same designs were used for solid chased coasters. The end of the Napoleonic wars seemed to mark a new age of grand silver—some of the massive (and often very ugly) plate presented to the Duke of Wellington bears witness to the sculptured silver-gilt display pieces. The classical permeated everything, and representational pieces translated Englishmen into Roman emperors graced by comely goddesses and nymphs. Flaxman designed a number of vases which were adopted for wine coolers, with Bacchanalian scenes in relief that must have caused much trouble to the silversmiths. But by about 1805 the simple half-fluted style with leaf-chased handles and gadrooned borders was too simple for the gilded banquets, and a deep applied band of vine leaves and grapes was the least a man of importance would demand for his coolers.

Tureens likewise showed all the many styles of the Regency. The graceful oval tureens of the last years of the 18th century, with their bat's-wing fluting and high reeded handles gave way to a Baroque style with bold scroll handles and heavy gadrooned rims. The circular or oval foot was often replaced by four massive cast leaf scroll or paw feet. But as with so many silverwares during the period, nothing remained in fashion for long—or everyone wanted something different. William Fountain could look across the Channel for inspiration from France even in 1806 and produce an oval tureen with applied decoration and a stand that scrolls into leafy end handles. In the same year Digby Scott and Benjamin Smith produced a pair of tureens, weighing 517 oz., with a deep band of vine tendrils enclosing rosettes and with a grand coat-of-arms in draped mantlings applied on either side. A few years later Paul Storr looked back to the Rococo, with a pair of immense tureens and stands, now in the royal collection. The oval bodies are fluted and applied with oak leaves—a Regency predilection—and have covers massed with fish, lobsters, broccoli, mushrooms and other vegetables. The stands are also

65. Candelabrum. 1819. Victoria and Albert Museum
London.

66. Two bottle coasters. 1810. The Worshipful Company of Goldsmiths, London.

65. Candelabrum. 1819. Victoria and Albert Museum, London. The Regency experimented with all the styles of the past. Sometimes quite unlike themes were married in efforts to create magnificence. Here formal foliate borders encircle the elegantly simple circular foot of this candelabrum, with its winged caryatid stem supporting a column with a classical capital from which scroll out foliate branches for the candlesticks, matching the foliate central motif.

66. Two bottle coasters. 1810. The Worshipful Company of Goldsmiths, London. Two of a set of four silver-gilt bottle coasters (or stands) made by Benjamin and James Smith. They are richly cast, chased and pierced with cupids reclining among vines.

67. Candelabrum. 1814. Height 37 in. The Worshipful Company of Goldsmiths, London. Probably of all Regency silversmiths Paul Storr is the best known. He spent many years working for Rundell, Bridge and Rundell, and among the many pieces he executed for them was this candelabrum, one of a pair weighing together 522 oz. The seven lights are supported on scrolling reeded branches rising from the central very simple fluted column, the base of which is a sculpted scene with cast chased models of Pan, playing his pipes, nymphs and goats. The base is circular and stands on four typically Regency paw feet interspersed with shells.

68. Entrée dish. 1792. Width 10¾ in. S. J. Phillips Ltd, London. This simple shallow entrée dish by Andrew Fogelburg and Stephen Gilbert has elegant incurved corners. The base has a gadrooned border, and the handle on the cover is formed as a reeded and foliate loop. The royal arms engraved on the cover indicate that the plate was originally issued to an ambassador.

67.

68. Entrée dish. 1792. Width 10¾ in. S. J. Phillips Ltd, London.

fluted and are supported on four tortoise and shell feet.

There were many revivals during the Regency. In 1814 Robert Garrard made a soup tureen in the quilted style, occasionally found in the 1750s. Sometimes Gothic tureens are found—such as a pair of 1800 by Paul Storr made for William Beckford for his Gothic house Fonthill.

Away from the leaders of fashion, the day-to-day products of the greater number of English silversmiths followed the grand Regency at a distance. It was no simple matter to keep pace with the themes that occurred and recurred—the lion masks in fashion one day, superseded by Medusa the next, the snake handles, the foliate ones, the simple reeded ones, the oak leaves and the vine leaves, lotus columns and anthemion borders, shells, scrolls, and all the figures of classical mythology that appeared throughout the age. The brilliant young men of the turn of the century—the designers such as Flaxman and Stothard, the silversmiths such as Smith and Storr—had established a style that was no one style, but all styles.

The silversmiths met the challenge of the designers, and were copied by lesser silversmiths. But the designers were primarily sculptors, and in following their whims, in making their models and working in high relief, the silversmiths had deviated from the traditional development of silversmithing. No doubt Storr and Smith, Philip Rundell and William Fountain could have brought it back to its slow-moving path. But by the late 1830s they were dead or retired, and the young men had been reared on the sculpture-rich silver of the Regency, perhaps without fully understanding the different styles that the great masters had harnessed into their own kind of order.

By the 1840s the old era was past. The patron was no longer a connoisseur who travelled on the Grand Tour, a dilettante and a man of taste among the classical ruins and in the studios of Italy. Europe itself was in ruins, rebuilding itself in the new age of industry. The rich man owned mines and factories, not landed estates and a place at court. It took more than one generation, more than one great war, more than a century for the silversmith and the designer once more to clarify their ideas and to find patrons to understand and want them.

The 19th century, with its tremendous impetus, its often execrable taste, its passion for craftsmanship and its incredible inability to put good craftsmanship into everyday things, did create a new genus—the collector of antique silver. By the end of the century English silver was considered worthy of studious attention. The collectors saved much for posterity, they helped to build up national and personal collections, and they found men and women ready to dig into the fascinating history of the hallmarks, the makers and the craftsmanship that make every piece, large or small, grand or simple, fit for a king or the little plaything of a country-lover, a worthy object of the collector's attention.

THE HALLMARKS AND THE MAKER'S MARK

Makers' marks and hallmarks are an invaluable guide to the provenance of English silver. There, in a few small punches are the indications of maker, place of making, standard of silver, and date. But hallmarks, taken too literally, can be a hindrance to the proper study of silver on its own merits. Furthermore, too much reliance on the marks may dupe the unwary into falling an easy prey to the faker or the unscrupulous trader who may try to pass off a poor quality work as fine, simply because the marks show a worthy maker's punch. But, with that caveat, it cannot be denied that the ancient system of hallmarking, with more than six hundred years of continuous use, has been a consumer protection *par excellence*, as well as, by chance, helping the collector of English silver to date and assess his wares.

Early in the history of silversmithing in Britain, and apparently also in most countries throughout Europe, the silversmiths found that a standard approximating to the sterling standard was most satisfactory both for silverwares and for the coinage. Pure silver is too soft to use unalloyed, but a small percentage of copper gives it durability without marring the colour. Sterling silver contains 925 parts of silver to every 1000—or, in Troy weight, 11 oz. 2 dwt of pure silver to the pound Troy. Troy weight is still used in Britain as the standard weight for gold and silver. The pound Troy contains 12 ounces (oz.), each ounce being divided into 20 pennyweights (dwt). One ounce Troy is equivalent to 31.10349 grams.

In Britain, all silver has to be at minimum of the sterling standard, and this has been so at least since AD 1300. Only one other standard is permitted—the higher Britannia standard, which is 958 parts per 1000 pure silver. This was obligatory from 1697 until 1720, and is still permitted and occasionally used.

Edward I in 1300 first ordained that the leopard's head mark should be used after any piece of wrought silver had been assayed, or tested. It seems that the leopard's head, now the town mark of London, was in fact originally the standard mark. Wares had to be assayed and found to be of sterling quality, and then marked with the leopard's head 'touch' before they were allowed to 'depart out of the hands of the workers'.

Half a century or so later, another mark was specified. This was the maker's mark. It was laid down in 1363 that 'each Master Goldsmith shall have a mark to himself', registered with the Guardians of the Craft who superintended the assay office. Often in those days, and indeed even until the end of the 17th century, the maker's mark was as often a symbol of some sort as his initials. Perhaps the symbol was derived from a shop sign, perhaps it was a pun or a rebus on his name. Today, unfortunately, few of these marks can be identified, and no written records exist at Goldsmiths' Hall relating the names of the makers to the known marks, until the surviving books start in 1697.

In 1697, the use of initials was made obligatory. Makers had to re-register their marks when the new Britannia standard came into force. The unexplained method was to use the first two letters of the surname —a most confusing practice, and only in fact made practicable by the addition of the symbols that were no longer used: 'Wa', for instance, might stand for 'Ward' or 'Wastell', 'Wi' for 'Willaume' or 'Wimans', and we should not be able to differentiate them unless it were for the small symbols incorporated in the punches. In 1720, when the sterling standard was restored, new marks had again to be registered, and the initials of forename and surname were stipulated. Many goldsmiths continued, however, to include symbols in their punches. The Huguenots, for example, liked to use the fleurs-de-lys and the two pellets such as were used in France; those supplying the

69. Silver-gilt tray. 1822. Width 22½ in. Garrard and Co. Ltd, London.

69.   Silver-gilt tray. 1822. Width 22½ in. Garrard and Co. Ltd, London. This massive silver-gilt tray, weighing 158 oz. 10 dwt, is typical of the grandiose Regency styles. The border is magnificently chased and pierced with medallion heads, vases, and leopards among vines within a formal foliate border. The handles are formed as intertwined snakes and the four massive cast feet have a pair of lion masks on either side of a bold foliate design. The centre of the tray is engraved with the arms of Poynder impaling Cooper for Baron Islington. It was made by Philip Rundell.

70.   Table centrepiece. 1824. Height 22 in. S. J. Phillips Ltd, London. Sea themes were the favourite expression of the Regency Rococo, both at Rundell's on Ludgate Hill, and at Wakelin and Garrard's in the West End. This centrepiece in the form of a huge shell is topped with the model of a triton blowing a conch and rests on three sea-horses, on a rocky shell and foliate triangular plinth, of which the feet are formed of turtles and coral branches. A similar dish belongs to Shrewsbury Corporation and there are a set of four soup tureens apparently cast from the same shell mould in the Royal Collection. All were made by John Bridge.

71.   Wine cooler. 1827. Height 11¾ in. S. J. Phillips Ltd, London. This, one of a pair of vase-shaped wine coolers, shows the Regency version of the Rococo. The wave-like chased bases rest on four intertwined dolphins amid shells and foliage. Reeded and bulrush handles on either side arise from triton's masks and the bodies are matted and spirally fluted with polished raised ribs between. Made by John Bridge.

70. Table centrepiece. 1824.

149

71. Wine cooler. 1827. Height 11¾ in. S. J. Philips Ltd, London.

royal family or ducal houses would add a crown; others, such as Pantin who worked at the sign of the Peacock, or Maitland at the Grasshopper actually placed a tiny representation of these above their initials.

The maker's mark, introduced in 1363, and the leopard's head mark appeared to be adequate forms of marking for the following century. But there were from time to time complaints about laxity in administering the hallmarking laws, and in 1477 an Act attempting to deal with such complaints charged the Goldsmiths' Company with ensuring that standards were maintained. This probably led to the use of the date letter system, which was certainly in full use by the last quarter of the 15th century. Each year a different letter is used to denote the year, and thus the Wardens of the Company were able to pinpoint not only the maker, whose mark appears on the silver, but also the year in which it was assayed, and therefore the assayer, should there be any question of the ware's not being standard. Letters are used alphabetically, and in London a 20-year cycle is employed (J, V, W, X, Y and Z being omitted). Elsewhere, various other cycles are used, and it is wise to study them in the guide lists published in various forms. Each cycle also has a different style of shield as well as of letter, providing a superb method of dating uninterrupted since at least 1478.

The same Act of 1477 ordered that the leopard's head should appear crowned. This further suggests that the mark was 'the King's mark' rather than that of the London Goldsmiths' Company. The leopard's head remained crowned until 1821.

The last of the four chief marks on silver first appeared in 1544. There is nothing so far known of how it came about, but it is likely that the Goldsmiths themselves chose the lion passant mark as a guarantee that the wares they marked were of sterling standard, at a time when the coinage was greatly debased. At all events, the lion is now used at every assay office in England as the standard mark (being replaced in Edinburgh by the thistle).

A fifth mark, showing the sovereign's head in profile, was used from 1784 until 1890. This indicated that duty had been paid on the silver at the time of assay. Duty had, in fact, been exacted since 1720, but the evasions and anomalies regarding wares not large or sturdy enough to take the punch had grown, and in 1784 the matter was settled by decreeing the additional punch. In recent years, the sovereign's head has been used with happier connotations—from 1933 to 1935 to commemorate the Silver Jubilee of George V and Queen Mary, and in 1952 and 1953 to celebrate the coronation of Elizabeth II.

Thus it will be seen that until about 1478, silver was marked with the leopard's head and the maker's mark. From then until about 1544 there were the leopard's head, the date letter and the maker's mark. Then in 1544 was added the lion passant, crowned at first, but from 1548 uncrowned and gardant. These marks were used in slightly varying forms until 1697.

The period of Britannia standard silver, from March 1697 until 1st June 1720, was indicated by special marks—the lion's head erased and the 'figure of a woman commonly called Britannia'. A new series of date letters was started with the new marks. This means that the letter 'a' only lasted from March 1697 until May, as the letter was always changed in May. The old sterling marks of the leopard's head crowned and the lion passant were restored in 1720, though some silversmiths continued to work in the Britannia standard, and their works were accordingly marked with Britannia and the lion's head erased. In 1821 the leopard's head, crowned for so long, finally lost it, but otherwise the marks remained little changed except for the shape of the shields.

The duty marks, like the other marks, varied somewhat over the years. In 1784 and 1785 the King's head was incuse, and faced to the left. It was reversed the next year, and appeared in an oval. The style also varied with each sovereign. When Queen Victoria came to the throne in 1837 the profile again faced to the left. In connection with the imposition of duty in 1784, a drawback mark (a figure of Britannia standing, incuse) was used on exported wares. As it was struck after the silver was finished, the danger of damage was great, and it was only used for nine months, from December 1784.

Outside London the history of assaying and hallmarking is much more chequered. Various towns were from time to time authorised as assay towns; others seem to have used marks, mostly based on the town arms, without special legislation. When the Britannia standard was imposed, the lawmakers seem to have forgotten about the provincial silversmiths, and it was not until 1700 that York, Exeter, Bristol, Norwich and Chester were specified as assay towns. Even then Newcastle was forgotten, and had to wait until 1702 for reinstatement.

Of the provincial centres, large or small, none of the old ones are now entitled to mark silver. The only British assay offices outside London are Birmingham (using an anchor), Sheffield (a crown) and Edinburgh (a castle). Birmingham and Sheffield were given their status in 1773, largely due to the petitioning of status, from 1819 at least, but the office there was closed in 1964.

The study of the marks applied either by the authorities or by the silversmiths as a sort of warranty of their own in the provinces is one of great fascination. Chester, York, Newcastle and Exeter had long-established silver industries. Norwich craftsmen were noted until about 1700, while silver is known from many other places, from Inverness and Aberdeen to Taunton and Truro, in Hull and Barnstaple, Plymouth, Leeds and Dundee, to name but a few of the better known silver towns.

Fascinating, too, are the pieces which bear incomplete marks. Often, it appears, by design or accident, silversmiths making to special order for a patron did not always submit their wares for assay, merely 'signing' it with their own mark. Some pieces are not even marked at all, but with a determined study of styles most pieces can with certainty be dated within five or six years. The changes in silver design come slowly and distinctly. Each age had its particular contribution to make, in design, in technique, in what it made. Even when the 19th-century craftsmen began to look back to earlier styles, they nearly always betrayed themselves in their work. For the most part, the mark of maker and assaymaster settles the question. When it does not, then the collector and the connoisseur can truly test his knowledge and appreciation of six centuries of English silver.

LIST OF ILLUSTRATIONS   Page

ACKNOWLEDGEMENT OF PHOTOGRAPHS

Antique Dealer and Collectors' Guide: 18, 44, 52, 59.

All photographs by courtesy of the Worshipful Company of Goldsmiths, the Ashmolean Museum, S. J. Phillips Ltd, Garrard and Co. Ltd, Harvey and Gore Ltd, and in private collections, were taken by Peter Parkinson, A.I.B.P.